STRUCTURAL AND FUNCTIONAL CHANGES IN THE JOINT FAMILY SYSTEM

STRUCTURAL AND FUNCTIONAL CHANGES IN THE JOINT FAMILY SYSTEM

(A Study based on D.C.M. Workers)

J.L. RAİNA

CONCEPT PUBLISHING COMPANY, NEW DELHI - 110059

The responsibility for the facts stated, conclusions reached and opinion expressed in this work is entirely that of the author and not of the Indian Council of Social Science Research which has financed the publication of this work.

ISBN 81-7022-237-0

First Published 1989

Jawahar Lal **Raina** (*b*. 1937-)

Published by
Ashok Kumar Mittal
Concept Publishing Company
A/15-16, Commercial Block, Mohan Garden
NEW DELHI - 110059 (India)

Lasertypeset by
Microtech Advance Printing Systems (Pvt.) Ltd.
H-13, Bali Nagar
NEW DELHI - 110015

Printed by
D.B. Offset Works
B-128, Naraina Ind. Area
NEW DELHI-110028 (India)

To my wife
for her
devotion and dedication

Acknowledgments

The present work is based on my Ph.D. thesis, thoroughly revised. In the preparation of this work, I have benefited from a great many people. I wish to express my gratefulness to all of them.

My greatest debt is to late Prof. S. Chandra who encouraged me to undertake this study and supervised my work for some time. I am also indebted to Prof. Chandi Prasad, Institute of Social Sciences, Agra University, Agra under whose supervision the work was completed.

Prof. Yogendra Singh, School of Social Systems, Jawaharlal Nehru University gave me invaluable advice and guidance at various stages of this work. I have benefited immensely from my discussion with Prof. Rajeshwar Prasad of the Institute of Social Sciences, Agra University, Agra. Prof. T.N. Dhar of Kashmir University and Dr. D.N. Dwivedi, Senior Lecturer, Ramjas College, Delhi University gave me much helpful advice and constant encouragement in preparing this work.

Mr. M.L. Saini (Dy. Librarian, Delhi University, Delhi) and Mr. Monga (Ratan Tata Library, Delhi) helped me in obtaining the necessary literature available in their libraries. I am grateful to them.

In completing my field work I received active cooperation and assistance from Mr. J.P. Sharma and his colleagues (Labour Welfare Officers, Delhi Cloth Mills, Delhi), which made my job smooth and enjoyable. To the respondents in the Mills, I owe deep gratitude.

I gratefully acknowledge the financial assistance I have received from the Indian Council of Social Science Research (ICSSR), Delhi, for the publication of this work.

I am thankful to Concept Publishing House, Delhi for bringing out this book efficiently in a short period of time.

J.L. Raina

Contents

List of Tables

ONE

Introduction

Family system has been one of the most prominent subjects in the sociological studies of Indian Society, particularly after nineteen fifties. Most of these studies are based on the premise that the traditional form of Indian family system was 'Joint Family' Their principal focus is to study the changes which this institution has undergone and to examine the present form of family system in India. Sociologists however arrive at widely divergent and conflicting conclusions regarding both of them.

A section of sociologists -(Ross, 1961:50 and Driver, 1962: 112-20)--is of the opinion that joint family system is disintegrating in India. Another section (Desai, 1955: 97-117 and Mukherjee, 1965:200) feels that the institution is as strong as ever. Similarly, there are conflicting opinions on its present form: "Iravati Karve suggests that it is the larger or smaller joint family that is typical of India; S.C.Dube, on the other hand, suggests that the nuclear family or small family is typical" (Kolenda, 1968:342). Such divergent views can be attributed to a number of reasons. First, there is no commonly accepted definition of the joint family: "Conceptually and operationally there have been confusions and controversies in the use of the terms elementary family and extended family even in the scientific sociological literature" (Ishwaran, 1974: 163). Secondly, different approaches have been adopted by sociologists and indologists for studying this institution. Lastly, in spite of regional variations in the family patterns in India, attempts have been made to make generalizations and to suggest the existence of a particular type of family in the country.

The diversity in the views of various sociologists is partly because the nature and characteristics of the various social groups studied so far are diverse. Shah (1973: 162) has observed that "there are many diverse social groups and there may, therefore, be many diverse lines of change". The diversity in views only proves that the question whether or not the institution of joint family is disintegrating remains unresolved. In fact, the issue will continue to be controversial until sufficient empirical evidence regarding the family system of different sections of our society is collected to get an overall picture of this institution.

Shah (1973: 173) also suggests that the phenomenon "should also be studied in different sections of society in different regions of the country, so that it may become possible to evolve an all India picture". This however does not mean that studies on the family system of the different sections of our society have not been undertaken. In fact, many sections of our society have been studied: e. g. teachers (Kapadia, 1955), villagers (Dube, 1955), business community (Agarwala, 1955), lower-income-group employees (Aiyappan, 1955), middle class urban residents (Ross, 1961), students (Shahani, 1961), town dwellers (Desai, 1964), and industrialists (Singer, 1968). However, a very important section of our society, i.e. the industrial worker vis-a-vis his family system, has not received much attention. Of course, quite a few studies on industrial workers have been undertaken: e.g. by Lambert (1963) and Strauss (1974). But these studies do not focus exclusively on their family system. Besides it would also be meaningful and illuminating in the context of changes in the family system. For we do not have a permanent industrial population in our country: it has a strong migratory character. Since the process of migration is likely to be accelerated further by ever increasing population pressure on land in the rural areas and industrial expansion in the urban areas the migration of rural population to the urban industrial centres is bound to increase in future. Such migration may not leave the family system unaffected. The influence of the urban way of life might change the attitude of the migrants, particularly of those who have either settled permanently in the urban environment or are in constant touch with the urban way of life.

Purpose of the Study

The present study aims at finding out whether the industrial worker adheres to the traditional outlook regarding the institution of joint family or whether the nature of his occupation and continued contact with the urban environment have brought about any change in his role-perception and responsibilities towards the kinship group. The major specific objectives of the study are:

(i) To study the existing pattern of family structure of industrial workers of a metropolitan city;
(ii) to examine whether the existing family pattern of the industrial workers conforms to the norms of traditional joint family and also to examine the nature and extent of change in it, if any;
(iii) to examine the existing family pattern in the light of the interactionist approach to find out whether families are functionally joint or nuclear; and
(iv) to indicate future trends regarding the joint family system.

Hypotheses

The study is conducted with a view to testing the following hypotheses:

(i) Since most of the industrial workers come from rural areas, our first hypothesis is that industrial occupation calls for physical mobility from rural to urban areas, and, therefore, the structure of family tilts towards nuclearity.
(ii) Establishment of nuclear families away from the paternal residence decreases the frequency of contacts, which weakens its relationship with other kinship group(s) and thereby, reduces the degree of jointness of the family.
(iii) An individual earner in an urban area seems to have a tendency not to share his fortune with other affinal relatives. Therefore, the degree of jointness in the form of fulfillment of mutual obligations is affected adversely by the establishment of a separate nuclear family. The longer the duration of staying away from the parent family, the lower the degree of jointness.

(iv) The joint family pattern is expected to be less prevalent in fraternal than in lineal relatives.

Conceptual Framework of the Joint Family

Since the present study is an enquiry into the joint family system of a particular section of society, and a number of varying concepts of joint family have been suggested and used in earlier studies, it is essential to discuss the relevant concepts to evolve a working concept for the present study. This section, will, therefore, be devoted to the discussion of (i) the various concepts of joint family--traditional and non-traditional, and (ii)the emergence of such forces as are said to be incompatible with the traditional concept of joint family.

Traditional Concept

One of the most authoritative and precise definitions of the joint family is given by Karve (1965: 8): it is "a group of people who generally live under one roof, who eat food cooked in one kitchen, who hold property in common, participate in common family worship and are related to one another as some particular type of kindred". Jolly (1953: 737), Kapadia (1966: 309), and L.S.S.O.' Malley (1976: 121) have emphasised almost the same characteristics in their definitions of the system.

A general description of this institution given by F.H. Das (1932: 99) includes the structural aspect of the joint family: "In the Joint family father, brother, their sons and all male descendents remain under the same roof. Girls taken in marriage are added to this group from outside, while sisters and daughters of the family in their turn leave it to be absorbed as wives into other families. All property except a bride's six fold property (mostly wedding gifts and ornaments) is joint property held under the unrestricted control and at the absolute disposition of the eldest male member of the family." Almost a similar definition has been given by Mandelbaum (1948: 93); he describes the joint family as "a number of married couples and their children who live together in the same household. All the men are related by blood as a man and his sons and grandsons, the women of the household are their wives, unmarried daughters and, perhaps, the widow of a deceased kinsman." These definitions emphasise some of the commonly accepted features of the traditional joint family: filial and fraternal solidarity, adoption of women through marriage, common purse, common property, mutual help and mutual obligations.

Socio-Economic Changes and The Emergence of a New Concept

Despite the fact that certain forces sustained the joint family system in its traditional form for quite a long time, the changing socio-economic conditions seem to have brought about a considerable change in the structure and functioning of this institution, which in turn has necessitated a change in the concept of the joint family. One of the most important factors responsible for such a change is industrialization: "The rise of industrialization affects all social units whose members become involved in serving industrial goals. Large, closely knit family groups disintegrate, giving way to more flexible and less committing nuclear families. Traditional family power collapses providing more freedom of movement for all family members" (A.J. Matejko, 1974: 146). The growth of industries and the increasing mobility of people 'weaken or even destroy joint family patterns' (Linton; 1952: 84). Industrial growth gives rise also to occupational and social mobility, which 'shatters the old social patterns' (Desai, 1955: 112) and affects the cementing bond of the family and the family changes from consanguinity to conjugality' (Desai, 1961:48).

Secondly, industrialisation leads to urbanisation and the growth of modern cities. Some of the attributes of such cities are: differentiation between kinship and occupational structures, monetization of the economy, possibility of occupational differentiation within the kinship group, level of technological development calling for extended and widespread education, greater secularization and an individualistic philosophy of life (Gore, 1968:47). These features of the modern cities are detrimental to the traditional form of the joint family. Besides, the development of urban centres encourages migration of rural people to the cities by offering alternative job opportunities outside factories, better educational and medical facilities, efficient and cheaper means of transport and communication. Migration of individuals or part of family and their establishment as nuclear units converted what once used to be a 'production unit' into a 'consumption unit', Stephens (quoted by Chekki, 1974: 208) has observed that "as industrial development accelerates, it should bring urbanisation, geographic mobility, rapid culture change and protracted schooling for the masses--which in turn, may be expected to lead toward American style family customs: a progressive 'isolation' of the nuclear family from the large kin group"

Thirdly, modern educational system has also contributed to changes in the institution of the joint family; through it individual develops initiative and drive, and it fosters the feeling of individuality in man. In doing so, it makes inroads into the foundations on which the institution of the joint family was based. To mention one, the age old hereditary occupation invariably compelled the younger generation to remain loyal to their elders for getting training in the required skills for their occupation. Their freedom from hereditary occupations rids them of their sentimental attachments with their elders. This is further strengthened by their contact with new progressive thinking in cities. Gore (1968:45) rightly remarks that the "Secularisation of life and the growth of individualistic philosophy are incompatible with joint family living because by emphasising the norms of rationality, the uniqueness of individual personality, and the individual's right to pursue his own goals, they make conformity to family tradition and acceptance of familial controls difficult for individual members."

Fourthly, the rising status of woman is also considered to be detrimental to the continuance of the traditional pattern of the joint family in India. In traditional Hindu society women held an inferior status in family as well as in society. They lacked personal freedom and had little or no decision making powers; they were governed by the elders of the family. Since they had no right of inheritance the chances of bifurcation caused by dissensions between female members of the family were reduced. But there has been a gradual elevation in woman's status due to the efforts made by social reformers, legal protection of their rights, the rise in their level of education, their higher marriageable age, the widening employment opportunities outside the households, and the gradual social awakening of the class itself. Such a change in their status has encouraged them to challenge the elders of the family and also to press their rights for equality and decision-making powers. This leads to conflicts and quarrels within the family, which inevitably lead to division within the family.

Fifthly, apart from socio-economic changes, the changes in the laws governing the family property have also adversely affected the joint family solidarity. These laws[1] (Kapadia, 1966: 262) have given the right to property to females and strengthened their legal position within the family vis-a-vis other members. This new power and position of strength has made them assertive and has very often contributed to the break-up of the families and division of property. Several legal provisions have also led to the breaking up of the family. "Hindu joint family particularly in the cities has been greatly influenced by the introduction of English Common Law" (M.A. Rauf quoted in Ross, 1961:26). "The Income Tax law and the new Estate Duty will go even further in disrupting the joint family". (Agarwala, 1955: 144-45).

Lastly, a relatively more important and, under the modern conditions, a more relevant factor is economic compulsion arising out of growth in the size of the family. The growing size of the family leads to a fall in per capita income, particularly in the rural areas, where the size of land holding does not increase along with the growth of the family, and other sources of livelihood are scanty. Under such conditions, it becomes necessary for some members to move out of the village and seek employment in cities and towns. This contributes to the breaking up of the joint family.

In fact it is difficult, if not wholly impossible, to locate families which conform to the traditional concept of joint families. Possibly because of this some sociologists and government authorities have claimed that the joint family in its traditional form has been rarer than what is commonly supposed: "Such a large proportion of small households (33 per cent in villages and 38 per cent in towns) is a prima facie indication that the families do not continue to be joint according to the traditional custom of the country and the habit of breaking away from the joint family and setting up separate households is quite strong "(quoted in Kapadia, 1966: 279-80).

This view is, however, considered to be erroneous because it is based on non-sociological considerations and does not pay sufficient attention to changed circumstances. Instead of looking at the joint family system from a static and fixed position it is more pragmatic to redefine it in the context of the changed social scene.

Non-Traditional Concept

Many modern sociologists do not, therefore, consider the traditional characteristics of the joint family, such as common residence, common kitchen, common place of worship, and common purse relevant and essential in defining a joint family. For, even in the absence of such features there may be jointness among the members of the kin group, and the joint family may exist in a different form. What they consider important and relevant from the sociological point of view is the interaction between the members of various households belonging to the same kinship group. Desai (1964) suggests that "if we are to be sociological in our approach we have to take up joint family as a set of relationships and a functioning unit. Equating residential units with one or another type of family, as is done in the census, placed undue importance to co-residence and common kitchen as dimension of jointness". After critically examining the approach of the census authorities, Desai (1956: 148) remarks that "the type of family is not to be determined by the fact of co-residence, commensality or the size of the group. It is the relationship between the members of a household among themselves and with those of another household that determines the type of that household." He, therefore, defines the joint and nuclear families on the "basis of social characteristics". To quote him again (1956: 148) : a household is " a nuclear family if it is composed of a group of parents and their unmarried children, or of the husband, wife and unmarried children, not related to other kin through or by property or income or the rights and obligations pertaining to them as are expected of those related by kinship", and a household is " a joint family which has greater generation depth (i.e. three or more) than the nuclear family and the members of which are related to one another by property, income and the mutual rights and obligations. The members may be related collaterally or lineally". Desai rejects the age old determinants of the nature of the family and emphasises the relations between the members of a family for determining whether it is nuclear or joint. It is in fact the 'level of interaction' and the 'orientation of the actions of individuals' which are to be considered as the most important criteria for judging nuclearity or jointness of a family : "if the actions are oriented towards the husband, wife and children group it should be understood as a nuclear family. If they are oriented towards a wider group then that is to be understood as a joint family". (Desai, 1964: 32).

Kapadia (1966: 305) also holds similar view: "Common residence and a common kitchen are desirable as external insignia but are seldom necessary to joint living in conditions prevailing today". Keeping in view the developments in economic, social and cultural spheres, it is difficult for a large family to have a joint residence and a common kitchen. In one's approach to this problem emphasis must, therefore, be placed "on the relationships of the constituent members to the head of the family and also on the generation depth of the group." Kapadia (1966: 305) rightly observes: "the family is not joint in the traditional manner and has rather the appearance of a nuclear family yet it may still have to be classed as a joint family".

Milton Singer (1968: 437), too, does not regard household size or composition, common residence or property as the essential characteristics of a joint family, and suggests that, from a sociological point of view, the family should be studied as a "network of social relations among persons related in specific ways". According to him a family is a joint family if "the individuals within it are disposed to discharge towards one another the set of rights and duties specified in their religious scriptures, legal code and customary usages. The presence or absence of joint residence, joint property, a particular set of kin etc... does not necessarily make a group of people a joint family, nor does its absence deprive the group of that status" (Milton Singer, 1968: 426).

Bailey and Agarwala have studied the phenomenon from the same point of view. According to Bailey (1960: 345-52) a family cannot be denied the designation of a joint family if its members do not live under the same roof, eat from the same hearth, or do not practice common rituals. The only distinguishing characteristic of a joint family is "common property". Agarwala (1955: 142) also states that it is not "essential that in a joint family all the members should stay at one and only one place and eat in one kitchen". Emphasising the social basis of a joint family, Nimkoff and Gore (1959: 27) have also observed that a joint family "emphasises primarily the relationship of father and sons or that between brothers".

All these opinions confirm that the criteria for a joint family should not be confined to a common residence or a common kitchen; the more important criteria, in the changed context, are maintenance of common property, relations between the members of a household with the members of other affinal households, and the fulfilment of mutual obligations. Taken in this sense many sociologists state that the joint family still prevails in India. Members of a family may apparently break away from the 'common roof and kitchen' in search of better job opportunities, to take care of property in other towns/villages, and to earn higher income to add to their resources for supporting other members of the root family. This separation should not mean that the members have broken away from the family itself, and have disowned their obligations towards other members of the family. On the contrary, it may help the family: "The 'branch family' migrating to the city moves for the benefit of the whole family where siblings, nephews, nieces, and frequently brothers or sisters-in-law join the urban household from time to time for schooling, medical treatment, or simply for a change of scene". (Gupta, 1976: xxxii).

Thus the modern concept is not only realistic and pragmatic but is also more sociological. For, what makes a family is not living and eating together of persons related through blood, but the nature of relationships that they maintain, the level of interaction with each other, and the orientation of their actions and behaviour vis-a-vis other members of the family. It is quite likely that members living away from the root family may interact more intimately with its members with a feeling of kinship and affinity. Also, their decisions and actions on such matters as the accumulation of property, performance of marriages, etc., and their general social behaviour may be in keeping with the interests of the entire kinship group rather than the interest of their nuclear group.

Conclusion

The non-traditional concept of the joint family is more scientific and useful in the context of changed conditions than the traditional one. It should prove more useful in the study of the joint family system of industrial workers, particularly in the case of those who come from rural areas and get separated from their root families. The present study investigates the nature of the family of industrial workers using both the traditional and non-traditional concept. For one group of our sample workers lives in joint households apparently conforming to the characteristics of a traditional joint family, while the other lives in nuclear households. In the study of joint households, we intend to apply the traditional concept and also the relevant connotations of the non-traditional concept. Nuclear households shall be studied in the light of the non-traditional concept.

Approach

As mentioned above, the basic objective of this study is to examine the structure of the family of the industrial worker and changes therein and also to find out whether or not it is structurally and functionally joint. For this purpose, the industrial workers' households have been grouped under different categories on the basis of their kinship composition. The household composition has been studied in the light of the traditional concept of joint family to find out whether or not the existing family structure of the factory workers conforms to the norms of the traditional joint family. Composition alone, however, is not an adequate and appropriate test of the jointness or nuclearity of the family, since it reveals only structural jointness or nuclearity of the families. We have, therefore, studied the structure of the family against the criteria of a functionally joint family with a view to determining the functional jointness and nuclearity of the workers' families. Finally, the households have been regrouped in three categories–Joint, Marginally Joint and Nuclear Families–on the basis of their degree of jointness.

The criteria adopted for this have been:

(i) functional relationship between the members of the family, including such aspects as
(a)disposition toward and fulfilment of mutual obligation,

(b)frequency and purpose of reciprocal visits,
(c) rendering/exchange of personal services,
(d)seeking advice and approval of elders;

(ii) authority patterns existing in lineal and fraternal relations on the basis of inter-personal relationships.

In studying functional relationship–criteria (i) the following have been taken into account: the willingness, the actual fulfillment of the obligations, getting an opportunity of fulfilling the obligations, reasons for not fulfilling obligations and also for not having willingness or having any sense of obligations towards the other members of the family. The same aspects have been studied also in the case of reciprocal visits, rendering/exchange of personal services and seeking advice and approval of elders.

In regard to criteria (ii) jointness of the family has been judged on the basis of the nature of relations between the members of the family, both lineally and fraternally. The lineal and fraternal relations have been studied separately. In the case of lineal relations, attempt has been made to see whether the authority of the father/head of the family works effectively on the son and other members of the following generation. In the case of fraternal relations, an attempt has been made to find out whether the authority of an elder brother is acceptable to the younger ones or not.

Another important factor which is said to be helpful in maintaining jointness in families is joint property. Unfortunately the sample workers had either no property or just a small piece of land or a house in joint ownership with other members of the family. Besides, the respondents owning land could not give the exact area they owned; some of them were unwilling to disclose it. Also because it was not possible to cross-check their responses, joint property as a feature of the joint family has not been included in this study.

In the absence of studies on these workers and because of lack of adequate empirical evidence regarding the family system of industrial workers in the past, we have relied on some authentic texts for the normative pattern of family system in the past and adopted the same as our base line data for comparison. This has the approval of many sociologists. For example, while attempting a comparison between the inter-personal relationships in the traditional and contemporary Hindu family, Dhirendra Narain (1970: 455) states that for want of "factual evidence of how people did in fact behave in the past.... I quote only from authorities in support of these normative patterns because a high degree of concensus prevails among the members of Hindu culture". In fact he even suggests that "in the absence of three generational studies in India... this perhaps is the only way of bringing in the three time dimensions of past (traditional norms), present (contemporary patterns) and future (by providing links)" (Dhirendra Narain, 1970:455). This study has chosen the past norm as the basis for comparison and assessment of the nature and extent of change among people who are working as industrial workers and living in a city.

Besides, this study makes a comparative study of the various aspects under different age groups, residential backgrounds, educational levels, duration of stay in the city, and nature of household to find out whether age-differentials and duration of urban stay and several other factors have in any way affected the attitude of the respondents towards the joint family system, this would be taken as an indicator of future trend.

NOTE

1. Hindu Law of Inheritance (Amendment Act) of 1929. Hindu Woman's Right to Property Act of 1937: Hindu Succession Act, 1956.

TWO

Research Design and Methodology

The Universe

The present study was conducted at Delhi, which attracts within its fold people from the rural areas adjoining the city and of the neighbouring states as well, to live and work in an urban atmosphere. Such a situation is ideal for studying the impact of the urban way of life on the outlook and attitudes of persons having a rural orientation, particularly in respect of family system. The respondents selected for this study were the industrial workers of a prominent textile mill in the city, which employs workers from almost all the states of India. This mill is situated at Bara Hindu Rao, approximately four kilometers away from the Delhi Railway Station. It was started with the establishment of a cotton mill at Delhi in 1889. Today it is one of the pioneering textile mills of the country employing about six thousand permanent and about three thousand temporary workers belonging to different regions of India.

The initial survey showed that the workers of the mill could be classified into three categories--permanent, quasi-permanent and temporary. Only permanent workers numbering 5,620 were chosen for the purpose of this study. Quasi permanent and temporary workers were not included because they had not permanently settled in any occupation in the city and were not sufficiently exposed to the influence of the urban way of life. They shuttled between the village and the city depending on (i) availability of free time from their traditional occupation i.e., agriculture, and (ii) the availability of vacancies in the mill. Temporary workers got entry into the mill through their relations or acquaintances working in the mill or by taking chances at the mill gate when the vacancies were advertised.

The Sample

Since it was not possible to contact all the permanent workers personally a sample of about 400 workers was made. While drawing the sample it was kept in view that (i) workers in different departments got fair representation, (ii) workers could be contacted personally, and (iii) the sample was large enough to allow inferences to be drawn about the entire population. The lists of workers were made available by the various departments. So it was also convenient to use the departments as strata and draw samples from each one of them. Considering the over-all proportion of proposed sample size to the total population (which comes out to be nearly 1/14) we decided to take a systematic sample from each stratum (department) with sampling interval equal to 14. Actual number of workers so selected was 394, slightly less than the proposed size of 400 because every department size was not a multiple of 14.

TABLE 2.1: **Distribution of Workers by Department and the Nature of Job**

S.No.	Name of the Department	Permanent	Quasi-Permanent	Temporary	Total
1.	Spinning	1270	414	154	1838
2.	Waste Plant	255	108	38	401
3.	Weaving	1545	805	255	2605
4.	Folding	526	96	58	680
5.	Dyeing	390	136	119	645
6.	Printing	99	26	68	193
7.	Winding	499	155	60	714
8.	Sizing	89	24	21	134
9.	Drawing	203	73	13	289
10.	Laboratory	47	4	3	54
11.	Engineering	437	110	65	612
12.	Watch and Ward	85	38	28	151
13.	Sanitation	36	28	6	70
14.	Misc.	139	7	3	149
	Total	5620	2024	891	8535

Besides, all the workers appearing in the sample could not be interviewed for such reasons as (i) absolute reluctance of the sample worker in responding to the schedule, (ii) some workers on the muster roll at the time of drawing the sample had retired by the time they could be interviewed, and (iii) workers having neither father, nor brother nor an earning son, and hence not being in a position to provide adequate information required for the present study were not interviewed. Departmentwise distribution of the sample workers is given in table 2.1.

Characteristics of Sample Workers

Statewise Distribution of Respondents

With its administrative and business offices, banking and other institutions, Delhi has attracted many industrial units which have to draw their labour force from the adjoining states. Delhi Cloth Mills has on its rolls labourers mostly from Delhi, and the states of Punjab, Haryana, U.P. and Rajasthan. More than half of the respondents (56.4%) belonged to U.P. mostly from the neighbouring districts of Meerut and Ghaziabad. A few workers in the sample were also from eastern districts of U.P., mainly from Gorakhpur and Varanasi. Of the remaining, about 21% of the sample workers belonged to two other states--Haryana and Rajasthan. Thus, the workers coming from the three adjoining States--U.P., Haryana and Rajasthan - accounted for three-fourths of the total sample workers. The workers belonging to Delhi (63) constituted a small percentage (16.0%). The remaining 28 (6.9%) of the total belonged to five other states of Punjab (10), Madhya Pradesh (7), Himachal Pradesh (5), West Bengal (4), and Bihar (2).

The distribution of the respondents is skewed in favour of mainly four states: U.P., Haryana, Rajasthan and Delhi. The study, therefore, pertains, by and large, to the industrial workers coming from these states only. Despite the fact that sample population includes respondents from other states, too, the number of such workers was very small to permit any generalisation.

Rural and Urban Background of the Respondents

Of the total number of sample workers, 333 (83.9%) came from outside Delhi and, by and large, belonged to the rural areas and the remaining 63 (16.1%) were the residents of Delhi. The distribution of respondents on the basis of rural and urban background is presented in table 2.2.

TABLE 2.2: **Respondents' Present Residential Pattern**

S.No.	Present Residential Pattern	Number of Respondents	Percentage
1.	Migrant-city dwellers	270	68.5
2.	Migrant-commuters	61	15.4
3.	Native-city-dwellers	45	11.4
4.	Native commuters	18	4.7
	Total	394	100.0

Present Residential Pattern of the Respondents

We have noted above that the majority of sample workers came from the adjoining states, and had mainly a rural background. When workers migrate from their native place to the place of work in the city they are exposed to the urban way of life in general and to the social life of their counterparts in particular. Living in an urban set-up is expected to change, among other things, their outlook towards the institution of family. Such a change in outlook can be brought about by comparing the outlook of native urban workers with that of migrants. For this purpose, sample workers were grouped under two categories – migrant and native.

Another category, which is common to both of these, consists of the workers who live in the suburbs of the city and commute between the place of their residence and the place of their work. On the basis of whether a commuter is migrant or native, this category of workers has been further grouped under two sub-categories: (i) migrant-commuters and (ii) native-commuters. The workers belonging to these categories are a little different from their counterparts living in the city, in the sense that they are not strictly under the influence of urban way of life as city dwellers, both native and migrant.

Keeping these considerations in view, the sample workers were grouped under four categories:

i. Migrant-city-dwellers,
ii. Migrant-commuters,
iii. Native-city-dwellers,
iv. Native-commuters.

The Migrant-city-dwellers comprise the respondents who have migrated from other states to Delhi to take up the present occupation and live in the city either in the accommodation provided by the employer or in a rented house which they got on their own. Migrant-commuters include those who have come from other states but live in the suburbs of Delhi in rented houses or in their own juggies, and commute to the Mill. The category of native-city-dwellers consists of those who have been living in the city since their birth, and live either in accommodation provided by the employer or in their own houses or in a rented one. Similarly, native-commuters include the workers living in Delhi since their birth, but in suburbs and commuting to the Mill. The distinction between the native-city-dwellers and the native-commuters is not only that the one commutes and the other does not, but also that the former is more close to the urban way of life than the latter.

Table 2.2 shows the distribution pattern of the sample workers between the four categories mentioned above. The majority of the sample workers fell in the category of migrant-city-dwellers. They accounted for 68.5% of the total while migrant-commuters accounted for only 15.4%. The remaining 16.1% subjects belonged to the category of native of which 11.4% were native-city-dwellers and 4.7% native-commuters.

Agewise Distribution of the Respondents

Since age is one of the most important variables which explains the attitude of the people towards the family system (Gore, 1968: 50), the respondents were divided into nine age-groups, each of five-year interval, except the first group which has an interval of three years. The age groups chosen were between 18 and 60 years (according to Factories Act 1948). Table 2 3 (column 7) shows that workers below 26 years and above 50 years of age have relatively smaller proportion in the same population: 8.3% and 12.8% respectively. More than half of the sample workers (about 56%) belonged to the age groups of 26-40 years. This may be considered as the model age group of the population. A little less than one-fourth of the workers were between 41 to 50 years.

TABLE 2.3: **Distribution of Respondents by their Age and Level of Education**

S. No.	Respondents' Age (yrs.)	Respondents' Level of Education Nil	Primary (1-5)	Middle (6-8)	H. Sec. & Inter (9-12)	College Education	Total (Age Group)
1.	18-20	-	-	3	1	-	4 (1.8)
2.	21-25	3	-	2	18	3	26 (6.5)
3.	26-30	4	4	14	50	2	74 (18.5)
4.	31-35	9	8	21	46	1	85 (21.5)
5.	36-40	14	7	20	20	2	63 (15.9)
6.	41-45	8	9	14	19	-	50 (12.6)
7.	46-50	11	5	16	9	-	41 (10.4)
8.	51-55	13	4	16	4	-	37 (9.3)
9.	56-60	5	2	5	2	-	14 (3.5)
	Total	67 (17.1)	39 (9.9)	111 (28.2)	169 (42.7)	8 (2.1)	394 (100.0)

This pattern of agewise distribution of sample workers did not permit generalisation, the workers were, therefore, regrouped under three broad categories: (a) younger age group, (b) middle age group, and (c) older age group. Under younger age group were placed the workers below 35 years of age (189) who constituted 47.9% of the total. Workers in the age group of 36-45 years (113) were placed in the category of middle age group, and accounted for 28.6% of the total. The rest of the workers, i.e., above 45 years (92) accounted for 23.5% of the total. These categories have henceforth been called as "younger", "middle" and "older" generation, respectively.

Level of Formal Education of the Respondents

The level of education is also considered as one of the factors responsible for change in the people's attitude towards the joint family system: "We would expect educated persons to be less in favour of, if not less conforming to, joint family norms" (Gore, 1968: 49). Therefore, with a view to finding out the difference in the attitude of the workers towards the family system, if any, respondents were classified (Table 2.3) on the basis of their level of education. Most of the sample workers seemed adequately educated for their position as factory workers. Workers having education up to secondary or intermediate level formed the largest proportion (42.7%) of the sample population and fell mostly within the age group of 26-40 years. A little more than one-fourth of the total respondents (28.2%) had education up to middle school level (between VI and VIII standard). These two categories accounted for nearly 71% of the total respondents. Another noticeable feature was that a considerable proportion of workers (17.1%) had absolutely no education; such workers were in almost all age groups (Table 2.3). Besides, only 10% of the workers had primary education. Workers having college education including one having a post-graduate degree in Sanskrit, formed a very small proportion (2.1%) of the total. Further, there seemed to be no co-relation between age and the level of education of the workers.

Duration of Respondents' stay in Delhi

As elaborated in Chapter I and also mentioned in the hypothesis (iii), the duration of stay of the respondent away from the root family plays a significant role in breaking the joint family. The longer the duration of staying away, the greater is the chance of establishment of an independent nuclear unit. We, therefore, studied the pattern of duration of staying away of the respondent from the root family and its possible impact on jointness. Staying away however does not mean that there is no communication between the nuclear household of the respondent and the larger kinship group: it only means that the respondent is economically independent and lives away from the "common roof" but keeps on occasionally meeting the other members of the family.

Table 2.4 presents the distribution of respondents according to their length of stay in Delhi. It shows that a majority of the respondents had stayed in Delhi for over ten years. Only about 15% of the respondents had lived in Delhi for ten years or less. About one-third of the respondents (32.7%) had been in the city for eleven to twenty years. Only the remaining 16% workers--the native--had been in the city since their birth. The table also shows that the majority of the respondents (about 58%) had been in the city for eleven to thirty years.

TABLE 2.4: **Respondents' Duration of Stay in Delhi**

S.No.	Length of stay (yrs)	Number of Respondents	Percentage
1.	Upto 10	58	14.8
2.	11-20	129	32.7
3.	21-30	99	25.2
4.	31-40	39	9.8
5.	41-50	6	1.5
6.	Since Birth	63	16.0
		394	100.0

Economic Background of the Respondents: A General View

In the foregoing sub-sections of the chapter we have dealt with the major attributes of the respondents, which, by and large, determine the outlook of the people towards the family system. Another important factor in this regard is the economic background of the respondents: it shows the extent to which economic scarcity or poverty works as a compelling force to make people move away from the kinship group in search of jobs. It is, therefore, pertinent to have a general view of the economic background of the respondents. Unfortunately, despite best efforts, adequate information regarding the past economic standing of the respondents could not be obtained. The respondents were not in a position to give even an approximate estimate of their parental income past as well as present. What they could tell at the most was the occupation of their parents. We are hence under a serious limitation of relevant data. Therefore, we have no alternative to relying on the occupation of the parents for bringing out only a broad outline of economic background of the respondents.

The highest percentage (47.9%) of respondents came from the owner-cultivator families. To know their economic standing we had to look into the size of land holdings and the size of the family, i.e., number of the members dependent on cultivation. Unfortunately, the respondents were not able to give precise information on this. However, the information provided by them indicated that the average size of land holding of the owner-cultivator could not be more than 3 acres for an average[1] size of the family of 6 members. Keeping in view that the size of an economic holding is normally considered to be 5 acres for a family of 5 members in the fertile region of the country, the average size of land holding of the worker's family is quite small. Since most of the owner cultivators have uneconomic holding they cannot be supposed to be economically well off, particularly when there is no additional source of income. About 8% respondents who came from the rural areas belonged to the family of share croppers and landless labourers. Families of this category did not possess any land of their own. They earned their livelihood by working on the land of other people as share croppers or as wage-earners. In both the cases their income is much less than their requirements as reported by the respondents. Much worse is the case of those who came from the families of village functionaries such as barbers, washermen, tailors and potters. Their income depended on their services rendered to the people of other castes. They got their payments either in cash or kind which was not certain and fixed. Of the remaining, parents of 14.8% respondents had worked or were working as industrial workers and parents of 11.2% respondents were serving as peons, clerks, shop assistants and class IV employees in the railways and the like. Industrial workers had a monthly income of about Rs. 400/- p.m. and those in other services earned between Rs. 300/- and 500/- p.m. or a little more. In both the cases per adult monthly income would be around Rs. 100/- p.m. This is by no standard a comfortable income for a city dweller. The economic condition of the self-employed parents as shop-keepers is no better than that of other classes. They mostly engage themselves in selling tea, pan, cigarettes, biscuits and vegetables in unprovided shops located in a corner of the house or in a kiosk. A few of them dealt in grocery; some ran small tea shops under huts on roadsides in the suburbs. Respondents reported that this class, too, could earn only a bare subsistence.

It may be inferred from the above description that most of the respondents had come from low-income families irrespecitve of the nature of occupation of their parents. It was mainly this economic necessity which had forced the respondents to take up factory jobs. This fact has been invariably mentioned by the migrant respondents as the main cause of working as an industrial worker in the absence of a better alternative source of additional income.

Tools for Securing Information

The Schedule

The requisite data were collected through a schedule combined with personal interview. The schedule sought information on the following important points: (i) the bio-data of the respondent, (ii) his familial background and the composition of his household, (iii) the behaviour of the respondent towards other members of his household and towards the members of other affinal households in this city, other cities, or in the village, (iv) his feeling and meeting of obligations towards the wider kinship group, (v) his interpersonal relationships--including relations between: (a) father and son, (b) sibling relations, (c) husband and wife, (d) mother-in-law and daughter-in-law, and (e) mother and son, and (vi) opinion on the institution of marriage and status of women.

Most of the questions in the draft schedule were provided with dichotomous responses of 'Yes' and 'No'; some of them were provided with statements and trichotomous responses to know the attitude of the subjects towards certain aspects of the joint family. Only a few questions were kept open-ended. The remaining questions were provided with alternative answers out of which the respondent was to choose one.

The questions included in the schedule were broadly of two types: one, those which related to certain facts concerning the actual family life of the respondent and, two, those which related to the opinions and beliefs of the respondent about certain aspects of the joint family which could help in assessing future trends.

The draft schedule was pretested on 10% of the sample workers with a view to judging the answerability of the questions and removing ambiguity therein, if any. This amounted to a preliminary investigation and was of great help in getting acquainted with field situations. Later, personal interview with some sample workers was sought through their section officers. On the basis of experience gained during the preliminary interviews, some questions, given the education of the sample workers, were found to be difficult for them to answer, and some did not elicit adequate response. Such questions were dropped and a few changes were made in the schedule, wherever necessary. The language of a few questions was redrafted and an effort was made to see that no question was left vague or ambiguous.

The data were collected with the help of the finally formed schedule by contacting the respondents individually in the factory premises or at their residences, depending on their convenience. While interviewing them the questions were explained to them in Hindi; things were explained to them wherever it became necessary. But care was taken to ensure that explanation and elaborations of questions did not encourage a biased response.

Interpretation and Analysis of Data

Responses to the single-response questions were tabulated first as a whole and then bifurcated on the basis of different variables (such as age, educational level, and residential background of the respondents) for drawing a comparative picture. The frequencies of answers in each category were converted into percentages. Open-ended questions could not be quantified so easily; answers to such questions were carefully analysed and classified in terms of specifically formed categories. The data were then analysed and interpreted with the help of tables.

In the case of multiple-response questions we tabulated the responses, not the respondent. In doing so we considered the preference for each option as a single vote assuming that the respondent had as many votes as the number of options. We then calculated the importance of each variable on the basis of its share in the total.

NOTE

1. **While calculating the average only those members who are dependent on cultivation have been taken into account.**

THREE

The Structure of the Family Units of Industrial Workers

The structure of the family units of industrial workers has been studied mainly on the basis of two aspects: (i) numerical composition, i.e., size of the household, and (ii) kinship composition thereof. We have then attempted on the question whether the existing household structure can be r garded as the present form of the worker's family, and also wheth the existing structure of family conforms to the traditional concept of the join family system or not. Accordingly, in sections I and II, we have analysed the numerical and kinship compositions of the households, and in section III, we have examined the household structure against the norms of a joint family. The analysis of the functional aspect of the workers' family i.e., inter-household relationships will follow in the next chapter.

I

Numerical Composition of Households

Following the household-classification adopted by Gore (1968: 12) and Shah (1973: 92), sample workers' households have been classified under ıour categories; small, medium, large, and very large. Households with 1 to 3 members have been considered as small, with 4 to 6 members as medium, with 7 to 9 members as large, and with 10 and more members as very large.

In our sample population (Table 3.1) nearly half of the respondents (49.5%) had medium-size households; 20.6% had large households; 18.8% had small households, and only 11.1% belonged to 'very large' households. Four households placed in the last category deserve a special mention. Three out of these consisted of 20 members each, and one respondent reported having 71 members in his household, who were all within the kinship group.

TABLE 3.1: **Numerical Size of the Respondents' Households**

S.No.	Household size	No. of Respondents	Percentage
1.	1 - 3 (Small)	74	18.8
2.	4 - 6 (Medium)	195	49.5
3.	7 - 9 (Large)	81	20.6
4.	10 + (Very large)	44	11.1
	Total	394	100.0

II

Kinship Composition of Households

The study of kinship composition is more meaningful than the study of the numerical strength of the households because it gives clues regarding the structural nuclearity or jointness of the families. There is however no uniform pattern of classification of the households on the basis of their kinship composition. Sociologists have adopted different patterns of classification in accordance with their requirements. Most prominent are the classification patterns adopted by Ross (1961), Kapoor (1965), Gore (1968), Kolenda (1968), and Shah (1973). However, none of these classification patterns suited our data. To find out the structural aspects of nuclearity or jointness of the families under study, households were first classified into two broad categories: Nuclear and Joint.

Nuclear Households

By definition, nuclear households generally consist of husband, wife, unmarried minor children, unmarried and unemployed minor brother, and widow mother. The last two are included in the category of nuclear households because they do not add to generation depth and are usually dependent on the male head (Gore, 1968; Kolenda, 1968). These nuclear households were then put into the following sub-categories:

i. *Uni-member Households*

The uni-member household consists of only one member, the respondent himself. Nineteen respondents (4.9%) in the sample population of 394 fell in this category. All of them were migrant-city-dwellers; only one was a migrant-commuter.

ii. *Respondent and Wife*

The number of households consisting of husband and wife was 21. Of these, 18 were migrants residing in the city, except one who was a migrant-commuter. The remaining 3 households were native. Households of this category have structurally broken from a larger kinship group. Some of the respondents in this category had separated from their parents or core family within five years of their marriage because of various reasons. A few others had separated because they could not reconcile with the idea of spending their hard-earned money on the children of their brothers or unearning siblings. One of the respondents, however, reported that his separation from the joint family was because of the ill-treatment his mother meted out to his wife. A detailed account of relationship pattern of this category with other affinal households is given in the next chapter.

iii. *Respondent, Wife and Unmarried Children*

The third category consists of the respondent, his wife, and their unmarried children. This is a household of two generations which is generally designated as a complete nuclear family. These number 229 and constitute 58.1% of the total. Looked at and on the basis of residential background, 75.4% of these are migrant-commuters; 56.6% are migrant-city-dwellers; and 33.3% of the native-commuters are living in such households. It can thus be inferred that more than half of the households are structurally complete nuclear families.

iv. *Respondent, Wife, Unmarried Children, Unmarried and Unemployed Minor Brothers and Widow Mother*

There is a good deal of controversy of whether households of this composition can be called a nuclear or a joint family structurally. Those who do not count widow mother in a separate generation consider such families as nuclear. Kolenda (1968) for instance, has included these in the category of "supplemented nuclear family". Gore (1968) too placed these in the category of nuclear families. Following these authorities, we have put such households in the category of nuclear households; their number in our sample population is only 13, which comes to nearly three per cent of the total. Of these, 8 are migrant-city-dwellers, and the rest belong to other categories. Younger brothers of the respondents are either undergoing training or searching for a job. The respondents, however, were very doubtful about these brothers staying with them after they would be financially independent and married.

Joint Households

The main factor which we have considered in regard to joint households besides living under one roof and taking food from the same kitchen is generation-depth. Our data revealed that many households were without any generation-depth though they consisted of employed and married brothers. Besides, some households had generation-depth as well as fraternal extension. Following these compositions of joint households we divided them into three broad categories, which were further divided into six different sub-categories. The three broad categories are:

(I) Lineally joint households,
(II) Fraternally joint households, and
(III) Lineally and fraternally joint households.

Table 3.2 shows that the first two sub-categories of joint households (i) and (ii) are lineally joint. The Households in sub-categories (iii) and (iv) are fraternally joint, and those placed in (v) and (vi) have attributes of lineally and fraternally joint households. Before we proceed further, a brief description of joint households is in order.

TABLE 3.2: Household Composition of the Respondents

S.No.	Household Composition	No. of Respondents	Percentage
	NUCLEAR		
(i)	Respondent alone - The uni-member household	19	4.9
(ii)	Respondent and wife	21	5.3
(iii)	Respondent, wife and unmarried children	229	58.1
(iv)	Respondent, wife, unmarried minor children, unemployed and unmarried minor brother(s) & widow mother	13	3.3
	JOINT		
	(I) Lineally Joint:		
(i)	Respondent, wife, unmarried children (including son(s) and parents)	22	5.5
(ii)	Respondent, wife, married son(s) and their children (including sons)	25	6.3
	(II) Fraternally Joint:		
(iii)	Respondent, wife, unmarried children, married brothers and their unmarried children	33	8.3
(iv)	Respondent, wife, and their children, widow 'Bhabi' and her children	3	.8
	(III) Lineally & Fraternally Joint:		
(v)	Respondent, wife, unmarried children, married brothers and their children, and parents	19	4.9
(vi)	Respondent, wife, unmarried children, married brothers with children, parents and grand parents	10	2.6
	Total	394	100.0

(i) *Respondent, Wife, Minor Children (including sons) and Parents*

These households consist of three generations and qualify to be called as lineally joint households. In some of these households, the respondent was the only earning member, while in a few others fathers of the respondents also earned something through self employment. Unmarried children were mostly minors and did not do any work. Fourteen of these households belonged to the category of migrants; 6 were native and the remaining 2 belonged to the category of native-commuters.

ii. *Respondent, Wife, Married son(s) and Their Children*

This sub-category too consists of three generations. The only difference between this and the preceding one is that the respondents in the preceding sub-category fall in the second generation and in this sub-category they make the first generation. In the households of this sub-category the respondent was the manager and head of the household. In most cases married sons were also employed and surrendered their salary to their father who gave them a part of it for their personal expenditure. In the remaining few cases, however, sons did not surrender their salary to the respondent but shared the household expenditure. The number of such households was twenty five (6.3%) of which twenty were migrant-commuters and five native.

iii. *Respondent, Wife, Unmarried Children, Married Brothers and Their Children*

This sub-category of households is only fraternally joint. The off-springs of the respondents and of brothers were all minor and unemployed. Such households numbered 33. Of these, 23 respondents were the eldest brothers and nominal heads of the household. In most households of this composition brothers contributed to the common pool of funds according to the size of their nuclear units. In case of occasional expenditures like the ones incurred at the time of marriage and death ceremonies, brothers contributed amounts mutually agreed upon. In very few cases salaries were handed over to the eldest brothers who managed the household. Barring one exception the households of this sub-category belonged to the category of migrants.

iv. *Respondent, Wife, Minor Children, 'Bhabi' and her Children*

This sub-category of households is also fraternally joint, though different from the preceding one, in so far as Bhabi, a widow, replaces the brother and is also partly dependent on the respondent. This sub-category is, however, not significant in our analysis because it accounts for less than one per cent of the total households.

v. *Respondent, Wife, Children, Married Brothers with their Children and Parents*

These are the households with three generation-depth, on the one hand, and of fraternal extension, on the other. In these households, parents had retired and depended on their sons. Fathers in most of these households were only nominal heads of the household. In accordance with their salary and responsibilities, brothers shared the expenditure. The position of the parents was subservient, as the management of the household was the joint responsibility of the respondent and his brothers. As reported by the respondents, there had been occasional arguments, in some of the households, between the brothers on sharing the burden of their parents. But households continued to exist as one unit under the force of circumstances.

The number of households in this sub-category was 19, which accounted for about 5 per cent of the total households. Of these 8 were migrant and the remaining native.

vi. *Respondent, Wife, Children, Siblings, Parents and Grand-Parents*

The households in this sub-category are joint in the real sense of the term. They consisted of four generations, but the respondents belonged to the third generation. Unlike other households, the management of this kind of household in most of the cases was the responsibility of the first generation, i.e., of respondent's grandfather. He, in consultation with his son i.e. father of the respondent, decided upon the expenditure pattern of the household. Two middle generations were the main income-earners. The womenfolk of the household shared responsibilities in order of hierarchy in the household. The number of such households was only 10 and accounted for 2.6% of the total: eight migrant and two native.

It is clear from the foregoing analysis that majority (71.6%) of the total households is nuclear. Only 28.4% households were found to be joint under six different sub-categories of joint households, those which have been termed as lineally joint are maximum in number – 47, followed by the sub-category of fraternally joint households numbering 36, and the remaining 29 are lineally as well as fraternally joint. In this way, nearly three-fourths of the households of industrial workers are nuclear and the remaining, a little more than one-fourth are joint on the basis of their kinship composition.

III

This section studies the family pattern of industrial workers on the basis of their household structures. This, however, raises a crucial question: can the existing household structure of industrial workers be straightaway taken as the form of their family? To put it more precisely: can a nuclear household of industrial workers be referred to as a nuclear family and a joint household as a joint family?

Classical literature "does not distinguish between family amd household" (Shah, 1973: 131). In several modern studies on the subject such as (Ross, 1961), the two terms--household and family--have been used interchangeably. In one study (Morrison, 1959), household-structure has been straightaway taken as a family structure without looking into its justifiability. Contrary to this, some sociologists have not only tried to distinguish between *household* and *family* but also have emphasised the need for making such a distinction: "When a complex household, say, of two or more married brothers, is partitioned, two or more separate households come into existence, but at the same time *a number of other relationships continue to operate*. They would cooperate in economic pursuits, hold and manage property jointly, help each other on many occasions, celebrate festivals, rituals and ceremonies jointly, and so on. This is also a normal process, which highlights the importance of technical distinction between 'household' and 'family'...Thus, *two or more households may be separate but they may* (emphasis mine) constitute one family" (Shah, 1968: 129-31). It is also true that exigencies of modern times create circumstances because of which "the members of a three-or-more-generational genealogical unit live in two or more households but are bound together by a number of activities" (Shah, 1973: 138).

On account of such situations the distinction between family and household becomes essential. Different related kins may be residentially separate but at the same time cooperating and bound together by different activities which are expected of those related by kinship. Household is, therefore, defined as "a residential and domestic unit composed of one or more persons living under the same roof and eating food cooked in a single kitchen" (Shah, 1973:

8), and family is conceived as "a set of relations and as a functioning unit" (Desai, 1964).

A distinction between household and family is much relevant in the study of family system of industrial workers, who under force of circumstances have, in most of the cases, to move away from the larger kinship group and set up a household in the place of their work. Such households cannot justifiably be treated as families. For, despite the fact that they have a separate household they may also be satisfying all other norms and codes of a joint family when viewed from the angle of functional relationships. For instance, the workers may be fulfilling most of their obligations towards other kinship groups and may also be coparceners in the joint property. This is equally true of people, other than industrial workers, who maintain a separate household. Hence, household cannot straightaway be equated with family and no worthwhile conclusions can be drawn, be it in the context of traditional or non-traditional concept of the joint family. We, therefore, intend to examine the household structure, both, nuclear and joint, against the basic characteristics of nuclear and traditional joint families, with a view to finding out whether a nuclear household can be treated as a nuclear family and a joint household as a joint family.

Nuclear Household and Nuclear Family

In this study we have followed Desai's definition of nuclear family with some modifications. According to Desai, "We can call a household a nuclear family if it is composed of a group of parents and their unmarried children or of the husband, wife and unmarried children, not related to their other kin through or by property or income or the rights and obligations pertaining to them and as are expected of those related by kinship" (1956: 148). We have modified this definition to include unemployed minor brothers and widow mother within the composition of a nuclear family[1], besides considering also a uni-member and also a household constituting of husband and wife only.

As table 3.2 shows, nuclear households have been grouped under four sub-categories: (a) uni-member households[2] (b) households with respondent and his wife (c) households with respondent, wife and unmarried children, and (d) the respondent, his wife, children, unemployed unmarried minor brother(s) and widow mother. Although these households definitely possess the compositional characteristics of a nuclear family, none of them however satisfy the other characteristics of such a family, i.e. not being "related to their other kin through or by property or income or the rights and obligations pertaining to them..." All the households of different sub-categories under nuclear households are related in one way or the other in such a way that the nuclear households appear to be only an extension of a joint family or only a part of a larger kinship group. For instance, all the respondents of uni-member households are married and have children, and are living alone not because they have severed their relations with their wives and children or their parents and brothers but because of certain other reasons; most of them have kept their wives and children at the village in the care of their elders. Besides, they pay frequent visits to their wives and parents. Thus, it is quite likely that a uni-member household, without having a common residence, and apparently looking compositionally or structurally a nuclear family--since it is categorised as one of the sub-category of nuclear households--is in effect a joint family. Similarly, with other sub-categories. In some cases of other sub-categories, the father of the respondent is alive but lives separately either in a village or in a city. In many cases, brothers maintain a separate household and live either in a village or in the city where they work or in some other city. Therefore, unless the inter-household relations are thoroughly examined, a final judgement on the nature of their family, i.e., whether they belong to a nuclear or a joint family, cannot be given.[3] These aspects are functional in nature and are examined in the next chapter.

Joint Households and Joint Family

In the case of joint households, it has to be noted that we are concerned mainly with the structural aspect of the joint family: to examine the structure of joint households with a view to finding out whether or not this structure satisfies the basic characteristics of a joint family.

Joint households have been grouped under six sub-categories having different kinship compositions. Two are lineally joint, two are fraternally joint, while the remaining two are joint lineally as well as fraternally. By definition, all the households termed as joint satisfy the structural or compositional characteristics either of a lineal or a fraternal joint family. Besides, all of them possess most of the characteristics of a joint family, such as, a common roof, a common kitchen and belong to the same kinship group, follow the same rituals and norms and worship the same deity, though only a few households have joint property. Households not having joint property do not possess individual property either. So far as generation depth--another characteristic of the joint family-- is concerned, except the fraternally joint families, all other sub-categories have a depth of more than two generations.

It can be inferred from this that since all the joint households satisfy all the basic criteria of a joint family, it will not be unjustified to regard joint households as joint families. It may thus be concluded that 28.4% of the total sample households are structurally joint families. Nevertheless, a family which is structurally joint may not necessarily be joint functionally too. And unless a household is joint structurally as well as functionally it cannot be said to be joint in the non-traditional sense. This question has been discussed in the next chapter.

NOTES

1. Their inclusion in the nuclear household has already been justified earlier.
2. As pointed out by Shah (1973: 143), the households of these two categories have, on the basis of their compositions, been regarded as 'irregular' (Nicholas, 1961), "non-familial (Mukherjee, 1962) or "families only through courtesy (Desai, 1964). We have included them (without giving any specific name) within the category of nuclear households or structurally nuclear families. This has not been done for having disregard for the anthropological definition of the composition of a nuclear family but because a part of their nuclear unit is in the villages.
3. Possibly it is on these grounds, in spite of possessing compositional characteristics of a nuclear family, Karve (1965: 137) observes, "it is not a *true* single family, because it has economic and ritual ties with a larger patri-family whose member the husband is".

FOUR

Changing Pattern of the Joint Family: Functional Aspect

This chapter studies the functional aspects of the family system of industrial workers. In section I we have tried to justify the study of this aspect and in section II, we have analysed the causes of the formation of nuclear households, their location, and their separation pattern. Section III outlines the criteria for judging the nuclearity and jointness of households. In section IV an attempt has been made to present an elaborate analysis of the functional relations.

I

The household pattern of the industrial workers on the basis of their numerical strength and their kinship composition have revealed that a vast majority (71.6%) of the respondents lived in nuclear households and only 28.4% in the joint households (Table 4.1). We also found that all joint households possessed almost all the traditional characteristics of a joint family. We, therefore, designated them as joint families on the basis of the traditional concept; what we need to do now is to assess functional jointness in the case of nuclear households.

However, a pertinent question arises at this juncture: can the numerical strength and/or kinship composition of a household be straightaway taken as the criterion for judging the nuclearity or jointness of families, and whether conclusions drawn on this basis can be valid? Many sociologists have strongly criticised the household composition as an adequate and meaningful criterion for determining the family type. Shah (1973: 3), for example, regards household composition as only 'one of the several dimensions of the family'. Desai (1964: 26) considers this approach non-sociological because studies based on this approach yield only "intolerably inaccurate and misleading" conclusions. Mandelbaum considers it as 'counting of heads clustered in a household' which can hardly yield a meaningful or valid information regarding the type of family.

TABLE 4.1: **Distribution of Respondents by Residential Background and Nature of the Households**

S.No.	Residential background	Nature of Household					
		Nuclear		Joint		Total	
		No.	%	No.	%	No.	%
1.	Migrant	247	74.6	84	25.4	331	100.0
2.	Native	35	55.5	28	44.5	63	100.0
	Total	282	71.6	112	28.4	394	100.0

The basic ground on which this approach has been questioned is that nuclear households may be only a unit of a joint family living separately for such reasons as (a) economic compulsions, (b) lack of accommodation, (c) forced migration, (d) better accommodation provided by the employer, and so on. Even if households are separated from their wider kinship group and are living away, it is quite likely that they are maintaining functional relations with other affinal households : "families may be structurally and residentially nuclear but functionally joint with say members of the unitary household in the city making regular remittances to other members in the village "Nimkoff and Gore (1959: 29). It is also quite likely that one household has branched off to the town mainly for the purpose of getting employment in a town and for supporting the parental household (Gupta: 1976). The household living separately and away from the larger kinship group cannot be considered as an independent nuclear family. Emphasising the importance of this aspect of family studies, Ishwaran (1974 : 163) states: "Paradoxically enough, both in the countries of East and West there seems to be woeful neglect of the study of the intricate interdependence of elementary and extended family..." M.N. Srinivas (1973: x) too observes :"Indeed, the whole subject of inter-household relations within a joint family is an important one."

It is, therefore, erroneous and misleading to designate a nuclear household as a nuclear family unless it is thoroughly studied in relation to its affinal households on the basis of the criteria of functional jointness. The same logic can be applied to joint households. As such, a household which is structurally joint may not be functionally joint, because its members or different units may not fulfil the functional criteria of a joint family. In view of this we studied joint households on the basis of functional relations between its constituent units.

II

Nature and Location of Households Related to the Respondents

Before studying the functional relations between the household of the respondent and the households fraternally or lineally related to the respondent, it is necessary to look into the nature, composition, and location of the related households, which refers to three categories of households: (i) households from which the respondent has separated and has formed a nuclear unit of his own, (ii) households which have separated from the respondent leaving him in a nuclear household, and (iii) households of brothers who upon having migrated to the city have formed nuclear households from the very beginning.

In all there were 282 respondents (247 migrant and 35 native) living in nuclear households (Table 4.1). Their distribution on the basis of the relatives from whom they had separated resulting in the formation of their (respondents') nuclear households and the relatives who had fallen apart and left them (respondents) in nuclear households is given in table 4.2.

The table shows that among the migrant (247), a large number had separated from the parental household: 112 respondents broke away from the parents and in 3 cases the sons of the respondents had separated. The migrant respondents who had separated from their elder brothers were 45 and in 11 cases younger brothers had separated from the respondent. In the remaining 76 cases, respondents first separated from their parents in the village, then came to live with their brothers in the city, but ultimately separated from them as well. In respect of separation between native respondents (35), and their relations, separation in 21 cases had taken place between parents and sons--14 respondents separating from their parents and 7 son(s) separating from the respondents. In case of separation between brothers, 8 respondents had separated from their elder brothers and in 6 cases younger brothers had left the household of the respondents, the elder brother, making their households nuclear.

TABLE: 4.2: **Separation Pattern and Formation of Respondents' Nuclear Household by Residential Background**

Sl. No.	Description	Migrant No.	Migrant %	Native No.	Native %	Total No.	Total %
1.	Respondents separat-ted from parents	112*	45.4	14	40.0	126	44.6
2.	Sons separated from Respondents	3*	1.3	7	20.0	10	3.5
3.	Respondents separated from elder Brothers	45	18.2	8	22.8	53	18.7
4.	Younger brothers separated from Respondents	11	4.4	6	17.2	17	6.3
5.	Respondents separated from Parents and brothers	76@	30.7	-	-	76	26.9
	Total	247	100.0	35	100.0	282	100.0

@ Respondents of this category first separated from their parents at village on different grounds and then from their brothers in the city on different grounds.

Cases of separation between parents and sons.

Causes of Formation of Nuclear Households

An important factor which largely determines the functional

relationships between the households after they come into existence is the cause behind their separation. It seems, therefore, pertinent to look into the causes which led to the formation of respondents' nuclear household. Out of 331 migrant respondents, 247 (74.6%) were living in nuclear households and the remaining 84 (25.4%) in joint households(Table 4.1). The separation pattern and the causes which had led to the formation of their nuclear households are discussed briefly.

Migrant Respondents

The causes of separation reported by the respondents have been grouped into three categories: (i) Economic causes--paucity of land and the desire to augment financial resources, (ii) Family quarrels and conflicts, and (iii) Inadequate accommodation. The distribution of respondents on the basis of the causes of their separation from their parents, brothers, and sons is given in table 4.3. Of the total migrant respondents 60.8% had migrated to the city mainly because cultivable land possessed by the then joint household was inadequate to maintain the growing members in the family. Respondents who migrated to the city in search of jobs with a view to earning additional income for the maintenance and purchase of additional land (even though land is adequate enough to maintain the household) accounted for 17.5%. Respondents of this category reported that they were disguisedly unemployed and thought it better to migrate to the city to take up a job and earn additional income. Those who migrated because they wanted to lead a separate and independent life and were apathetic towards agricultural occupation constituted only 4.8% of the respondents most of whom were semi-educated. In all 83.1% respondents migrated to the city directly or indirectly because of economic causes. This supports our hypothesis that '...industrial occupation calls for physical mobility from rural to urban area and, therefore, the structure of the family tilts towards nuclearity'. It needs to be mentioned here that all the cases of migration had taken place under a congenial atmosphere and with the blessings of elders in the family.

In the city joint households had broken up mainly because of family quarrels and conflicts; two major causes being frequent clashes between members of the household, particularly between female members, and undue demands on the salary of the respondents. The underlying factors were reported to be the differences in income and differences in the number of children in the nuclear units and clashes in the mutual expectations of the members and the

TABLE 4.3: **Causes and Pattern of Separation (Migrant Respondents)**

Sl. No.	Causes of Separation	Separation between Respondent and: Parents* only	Brothers only	Parents and Brothers	Total	%	
		1	2	3	4	5	6
	Splits in the Village						
I	Economic causes:-						
(i)	Inadequate land and other sources of income		70	16	64	150	60.8
(ii)	Additional income though adequate land		29	6	8	43	17.5
(iii)	Desire for better and economically independent living		6	2	4	12	4.8
		105	24	76	205		
	Splits in the City						
II	Family quarrels and conflicts:-						
(i)	Clash	2	14	32	16	6.5	
(ii)	Undue demand	2	10	27	12	4.8	
(iii)	Undue interference	3	4	8	7	2.8	
		7	28	67	35		
III	Inadequate accomodation	3	4	9	7	2.8	
	Total I + II + III	115*	56	76	247	100.0	

* Includes three cases where sons have separated from the respondents.

Note- Respondents in column 4 separated first from parents in the village due to causes in (I) and then separation between them and their brothers in the city took place due to causes in (II) and (III). They have been counted only once in the total.

respondent. Respondents who had separated from their parents or brothers reported the cause of separation as undue demand on their salary by their parents or elder brothers. But, where respondent's son(s) or brother(s) had broken away, the respondents attributed the separation to unwillingness of the former (brother and sons) to share the existing or expected responsibilities of the respondent. These account for only 11.3% cases of separation between households. But if we add to this the respondents (59) who initially migrated to the city leaving their parents at village, and later separated from brothers with whom they were putting up in the city, their percentage rises to 35.1. It seems, the separation between the respondents and parents/brothers living in the village was mainly because of migration due to economic factors, but separations in the city took place mainly because of quarrels and conflicts between the members of the household. Besides, these causes seem to be much more relevant in the case of separation between brothers. Out of 87 cases of separation on these grounds, 83 (95.4%) took place between brothers. It was reported that the quarrels between Jaithanis and Deoranis caused break-up of fraternally joint households.

The other causes which were reported to be responsible for the separation of households are undue interference by the elders of the respondent or by the respondent himself in the personal affairs of their younger brothers and sons and inadequate accommodation. The number of households which had separated due to inadequate accommodation were 16 (2.8%); out of this 13 had separated from their elder brothers and only 3 had separated from their fathers, while splits in case of remaining 2.8% had taken place due to the undue interference of elders.

Thus the formation of nuclear households was due to the break-up of both lineal and fraternal groups and the major causes of structural 'nucleation' of households were inadequacy of means of livelihood in the village, frequent clashes between female members of the household, and undue demands on the salary of the respondent.

Native Respondents

Table 4.4 presents the causes of formation and the pattern of separation of the native respondents in nuclear households. Out of 63 native respondents, 35 (55.5%) lived in nuclear households

TABLE 4.4: **Causes and Pattern of Separation (Native Respondents)**

S. No.	Causes of Separation	Respondent separated from parents	Son separated from Respondent	Total	Respondent separated from Brothers	Brother separated from Respondent	Total	Total	Percentage
	1	2	3	4	5	6	7 (5+6)	8 (4+7)	9
1.	Unwillingness to share family responsibilities	5	3	8	3	2	5	13	37.1
2.	Clash among women	4	2	6	3	1	4	10	28.5
3.	Insistence by wife	3	2	5	-	-	-	5	14.2
4.	Inadequate accomodation	2	-	2	1	-	1	3	8.8
5.	Exploitation and undue interference by Parents/ Brothers	-	-	-	1	1	2	2	5.7
6.	Government accomodation	-	-	-	-	2	2	2	5.7
	Total	14	7	21	8	6	14	35	100.0
	Percentage	(40.0)	(20.0)	(60.0)	(22.8)	(17.2)	(40.0)		(100.0)

(Table 4.1). Of these 60% separations had taken place between parents and sons. In 14 cases (40%) respondents had separated from parents and in 7 cases (20%) they had been left in nuclear households after their son(s) had separated from them. In the remaining 14 cases (40%) separations had taken place between brothers. Eight respondents (22.8%) had separated from their elder brothers and in 6 cases (17.2%) respondents had been left in nuclear household by their younger brother(s).

An enquiry into the causes of separation revealed a variety of reasons for the separation of households (Table 4.4). The most important ones seemed to be (i) the unwillingness of son(s) or brother(s) to share the responsibilities of the respondents and (ii) the frequent clashes between the women-folk of the households, particularly between respondent's mother and his wife and the wives of the brothers (i.e., between Jaithani and Deorani). These two accounted for separation of about 66% of the native respondents. In regard to the cases of separation due to the unwillingness of brother and sons to share the household responsibilities, the respondents reported that they spent their hard-earned incomes on bringing up and educating their brothers and sons. But when they got jobs and were married they showed reluctance to cooperate with the respondent in maintaining the household and prefered to spend their income on themselves.

This had bred conflict and tension and very often an exchange of hot words among the members, which ultimately led to the bifurcation of the household. The quarrels between female members of the household had been mainly on sharing the household chores. Mothers-in-law (wives of the respondents) resented the unwillingness of daughters-in-law to do household work like cleaning utensils and keeping the household in order. In case of Jaithanis and Deoranis, the latter were reported to have insisted on working less because their own nuclear unit was relatively small. When the frequency of such quarrels increased, the solution was sought in the bifurcation of the household.

Another cause of separation was the insistence of daughters-in-law to live separately and independently. Respondents reported that their wives could not put up with their mothers. They often quarreled and when things became intolerable, the respondent thought it better to break away from his father's family--the family of orientation--for the respondent. In several cases the respondents reported that their son(s) were in connivance with their daughter(s)-in-law. Separations due to this reason accounted for 14.2%.

In three cases (8.8%) separation had been caused due to inadequate accommodation shared by the respondent–two respondents sharing the accommodation of parents and one of the elder brother. Separation had become inevitable when the respondents were married and had their own children. But such separations did not take place under unpleasant conditions.

In two cases (5.7%) of separations, one took place as a result of exploitation and 'undue' interference of the elder brothers. In one case the respondent categorically stated that he separated because he was exploited by his elder brother. Another respondent reported that his younger brother had left him because his (respondent's) interference was considered 'undue' by his brother, although the respondent had objected to his activities like going frequently to the movies and having outings, coming home late in the night, and having associations with bad characters of the locality. In the two remaining cases (5.7%) joint households got bifurcated because one of the brothers shifted to the house provided by the Government.

It is noteworthy that while separations in the past took place usually due to the problem of accommodation under one roof (Karve, 1965), now separations take place because of conflicts and quarrels between the members of the family. Such separations may be taken as an indicator of the future trends in the joint family system.

III

Functional Aspects

For studying the functional aspects of households, both nuclear and joint, we have followed the interactionist approach[1] which emphasises inter-household and inter-personal relationships. The major questions to which we have addressed ourselves are:

(a) Whether 'nucleation' of the nuclear households is merely an extension of the joint family or whether there is functional 'nucleation' as well, and
(b) Whether households looking apparently joint are joint functionally as well?

In other words, we intend to study the nuclearity of nuclear households and jointness of the joint households with a view to ascertaining the family pattern of the industrial workers. Our attempt is to see whether nuclear households (categories given in Chapter III) have completely broken away from, or whether they still continue to have effective functional relations with those from whom they have separated. For this purpose, we have tried to examine the degree of intimacy of the respondents with their related households on the basis of functional criteria. These are four and have been drawn from the non-traditional concept of joint family:

A. Feeling and fulfillment of financial obligations,
B. Reciprocal visits,
C. Seeking advice and approval of elders, and
D. Rendering/Exchange of personal services.

On the basis of these criteria, nuclear households were grouped under the following three categories showing the degree of intimacy between the lineally and fraternally related households.

i. Closely related,
ii. Marginally related , and
iii. Nuclear.

The major attributes of these categories are:

Closely related: Nuclear households fulfilling following conditions were placed in this category.

(a) meeting financial obligations willingly, without expecting any return,
(b) having frequent meetings with each other,

(c) consulting each other in matters pertaining to the choice of spouses, negotiating marital relations, purchase and sale of property, and honouring the advice of elders, and
(d) obligatory rendering of personal services on occasions of marriage, delivery, and illness.

Marginally related: In this category are included households which fulfilled the following conditions:

(a) financial help is neither expected nor given. Fulfillment of financial obligations, if at all, is on reciprocal basis,
(b) infrequent visits or meetings–only on occasions of marriage or death and making social calls on reciprocal basis,
(c) formal consultation on matters given in (I) c, and
(d) rendering personal services being a matter of convenience.

Nuclear: Households not fulfilling the conditions laid down for closely related and marginally related households were placed in this category. This, however, does not mean that households of this category did not maintain any kind of relation with the other households. They did maintain casual and formal contact but neither expected nor fulfilled any monetary obligations. Besides, they did not render personal services nor did they consult each other on family matters.

In determining the criteria for judging the closeness or jointness between two households, we have tried to proceed in order of importance of the various aspects of inter-household relations. Which aspect is more important than the others is however a matter of one's own judgement. Besides, it also depends on the social norms observed by the households. One could even go further and say it is not the aspect which is important, but the spirit and the intensity of willingness with which households fulfill their mutual obligations and pay visits or consult each other on important matters. Unfortunately, no tool could be evolved to assess the intensity of spirit and willingness of the respondents in fulfilling their mutual obligations or helping each other. Nor could we know the intention behind the visits, particularly where expectations of reciprocity and selfish motives were suspected. Therefore, the order of importance of various functional aspects was summarily determined in accordance with the importance attached to a particular aspect by the respondent during the interview.

The study of respondent's functional relationships with his relations was intended to be done by taking the respondent in the capacity of a son and in the capacity of a father. But only 10 cases of respondents living in nuclear households had major and employed sons living separately within the city. The number being small, no significant conclusion could be drawn from their analysis. We therefore concentrated on the respondent in the capacity of a son, in our study of functional relationship. The 10 cases have been considered in the study of inter-personal relationship, particularly, between father and son.

IV

Functional Relations: Respondents' Households V/S Other Related Households

In studying functional relations, we covered the following major aspects:

A. Feeling and fulfillment of financial obligations,
B. Reciprocal visits,
C. Seeking advice and approval of elders, and
D. Rendering/Exchange of personal services.

Since only (A) is relevant to joint households, they were studied only in regard to financial obligations i.e. the pattern of sharing financial burden of the family by the constituent units.

NUCLEAR HOUSEHOLDS

(A) Financial Obligations

Financial obligations are the most important aspect in almost all kinds of human relations: especially so in the relationship between households joined by ties of blood. Desai (1964: 33) has very rightly emphasised the fulfillment of mutual obligations in the jointness of households. The major aspects of financial obligations considered in this study are: (i) whether respondents felt financial obligations towards their parents and brothers, (ii) whether they were fulfilled, (iii) the reasons for non-fulfillment despite a feeling to do so, (iv) occasions and extent of financial help provided, (v) whether fulfillment was done willingly, (vi) whether a return was expected, and (vii) financial help sought by the respondent.

Feeling of Financial Obligations

To find out the attitude of the respondents regarding financial obligations towards their parents and brothers living separately, they were asked one question: "Do you think providing financial help to parents and brothers, even if they are living separately, is a moral binding"? All the respondents, irrespective of their age, caste, educational background, earlier residential background, and with parents alive or dead, responded in the affirmative--probably because the question was too general. However, when the respondents were asked whether they had a feeling of financial obligations towards their parents and brothers, the response was some what different: many respondents (74–11 in case of parents and 63 in case of brothers) responded negatively (Table 4.5). It is worthwhile to note here that among the respondents who expressed having a feeling of financial obligation towards their parents 80 had lost their parents. A few of them described the father-son relationship as the only relation in which selfishness had no place and, therefore, should be maintained at all costs. Several others mostly from the older age group went to the extent of condemning the new generation and the modern way of life because they, ignored their responsibilities towards parents.

What is important in this regard is the response of those whose parents were alive, because they are more valuable than the responses of people who have no parents. The responses of this category of respondents regarding the feeling of financial obligations towards parents and brothers have been tabulated in table 4.5.

The table shows that a vast majority of respondents (94.5%) reported having a feeling of financial obligations towards their parents, while only 56.8% had this feeling towards brothers. These figures indicate that the feeling of financial obligations between the

TABLE 4.5: **Feeling of Financial Obligation towards Parents and Brothers by Respondent's Residential Background**

S. No.	Type of Relationship	Do you have feeling of financial obligation								
		Migrant			Native			TOTAL		
		Yes	No	Total	Yes	No	Total	Yes	No	Total
1		2	3	4	5	6	7	8	9	10
1.	Parents	182	6	188*	9	5	14*	191	11	202
		(96.8)	(3.2)	(100.0)	(64.3)	(35.7)	(100.0)	(94.5)	(5.5)	(100.0)
2.	Brothers	79	53	132@	4	10	14@	83	63	146
		(59.9)	(40.1)	(100.0)	(28.6)	(71.4)	(100.0)	(56.8)	(43.2)	(100.0)
	Total	261	59	320	13	15	28	274	74	348

Note: * Parents of only 202 respondents (188 migrants and 14 natives) are alive and living separately.
@ Brothers of only 146 respondents (132 migrants and 14 natives) are living separately.

lineal group exists in a much larger degree than in fraternal groups. Besides, the feeling of financial obligations towards parents and brothers also varied in accordance with whether a respondent was migrant or native. 96.8% migrants had a feeling of financial obligations towards parents: the corresponding percentage for native was only 64.3. Regarding brothers, against about 60% migrants having the feeling of financial obligations, only 28.6% native respondents reported having a similar feeling.

Respondents not Having Feelings

Out of 202 respondents whose parents were alive, 11 (5.5%) reported not having any feeling of financial obligation towards their parents. Similarly, out of 146 respondents having brothers living separately, 63 (43.2%) reported that they did not feel any financial obligations towards their brothers. The percentage of respondents (5.5%) not feeling financial obligations towards parents was too small to reveal a meaningful trend.

Moreover, all the 11 respondents having no feeling of financial obligation towards their parents were further probed to get at the reasons behind such an attitude. Our enquiry revealed that these lay mostly in the reasons for separation between the households. Most of these respondents had left the parental household either because of the huge responsibilities that their parents had or because of frequent clashes between respondents' wives and mothers, or on account of undue interference with personal liberties of the respondent. The relations between respondents and their parents in all the 11 cases were far from cordial; separations had taken place under very uncongenial conditions. This had made them indifferent towards their parents. Incidentally, most of the respondents of this category belonged to the younger age group and were either graduates or had left the colleges while studying for graduation.

All of them blamed their parents for this attitude of theirs (respondents): elderly people had failed to appreciate the changing times and wanted complete subjugation of the younger generation which they reported was not possible after one was married and had one's own growing responsibilities. The following notable facts regarding this category of respondents can be drawn from the above descriptions: (i) all the respondents of this category belong to the youngest age-group of sample workers, (ii) Ten out of 11 had separated from their parents in the city, (iii) the major reasons for their separation were (a) unwillingness to share responsibilities of their parents, (b) quarrels between mothers-in-law and daughters-in-law; and (iv) exposure to college education. These facts again do not reveal much about the future trend for the simple reason that their number is small. But this group along with its characteristics placed against the following expected trends in the society becomes meaningful. First, with the growth of industrialisation the number of industrial workers, both migrant and native, is likely to increase in the younger age group. Secondly, workers of this group are expected to be relatively more educated. Finally, migrants in particular, would come under the influence of the urban way of life which may bring a change in their attitude towards members outside their nuclear unit. If one considers these likely events in the light of features of the group not having a feeling of financial obligations, one would not be wrong in inferring that this group may increase in future.

Contrasted with the respondents (5.5%) who have no feeling of financial obligation towards parents, the respondents having no such feeling towards brothers accounted for a much larger percentage (43.2%). As in the case of parents, the feeling of financial obligation towards brothers also varied in accordance with whether a respondent was migrant or native: migrant respondents showing indifference towards their brothers were only 40% of the total migrants having brothers, while corresponding percentage amongst the native was 71.4.

Reasons for this are quite revealing. 67.4% migrant respondents did not have any feeling because they thought that their brothers' separate household was self sufficient. However, they immediately added that they were not in a position to give any financial help to their brothers, and as such there was no point in having any feeling for them. About 23% of the respondents did not have any feeling for their brothers because their relations were uncordial and had separated on account of bickerings between females. A relatively smaller percentage (9.5%) had no feeling towards their brothers because they had failed to return their money especially when they needed it. Among the native respondents 60% reported uncordial relations as the major cause of their having no feeling of financial obligation towards brothers. Twenty per cent each had no feeling for the other two reasons.

In all, 60.3% respondents did not have the feeling of financial obligation towards their brothers because they felt that the latter's unit was self sufficient. A little less than one-third did not have such a feeling because of uncordial relations. These two reasons account for about 89% respondents not having feeling of financial obligation towards brothers, and may be taken as an indicator of the weakening affinity between brothers.

Like the respondents not having feeling of financial obligations towards parents, those not feeling it obligatory to help brothers financially belong mostly to the younger age-group. About 74% of the respondents of this category belonged to the age-group 18 to 35 years. Migrant constituted a large percentage, i.e., 77.3 per cent while the corresponding percentage of native in this was only 60. Age in this way seems to be an important factor in determining the feeling of financial obligations towards parents and brothers.

Fulfillment of Financial Obligations

Not relying on sentiment alone, we tried to find out how much of it really became a part of respondents behaviour by studying their fulfillment of financial obligations, and took the following considerations into account:

i. Whether the respondents having a feeling of financial obligation had got an occasion to fulfil it;
ii. how many of these who had got the opportunity translated their feeling into action and what was the reason for those who could not do so;
iii. whether those who fulfilled the obligation did so willingly and without expectation of reciprocity;
iv. whether the fulfillment was in accordance with the expectations or demands from the relations, particularly when the money remitted was for their benefit?

The information regarding the first two questions is presented in Table 4.6. It yields the following conclusions:

TABLE 4.6 : **Distribution of Respondents Having Feeling, getting opportunity and fulfilling Financial Obligation towards Parents and Brothers by their Residential Background**

	Migrant							Native							Total						
Type of Relationship	Total *	Having Feeling	% of col.3 to col.2	Having got oppor-tunity	% of col.5 to col.3	Fulfill-meat	% o col.7 to col.5	Total*	Having Feeling	% of col.10 to col.9	Having got oppor-tunity	% of col.12 to col.10	Fulfill-meat	% of col.14 to col.12	Total*	Having Feeling	% of col.17 to col.16	Having got Oppor-tunity	% of col.19 to col.17	Fulfill-meat	% of col.21 to col.19
1	2	3	4	5	6	7	8	9	10	11	12	13	14	15	16	17	18	19	20	21	22
Parents	188*	182	96.8	158	86.8	142	89.8	14*	9	64.2	6	66.6	6	100.0	202*	191	94.5	164	85.8	148	90.2
	-	(96.8)	-	(84.1)	-	(75.5)	-	-	(64.2)	-	(42.8)	-	(42.8)	-	-	(94.5)	-	(81.1)	-	(73.2)	-
Brothers	132@	79	59.8	57	74.7	49	85.9	14@	4	28.5	2	50.0	2	100.0	46@	83	56.8	59	(71.0)	31	84.7
	-	(59.8)	-	(43.2)	-	(37.1)	-	-	(28.5)	-	(14.3)	-	(14.3)	-	-	(56.8)	-	(40.4)	-	(34.9)	-

* Figures refer to the respondents having their parents alive and living separately.

@ Figures refer to the respondents whose brothers are living separately.

Note: Figures in the paranthesis are percentage to totals in cols. 2, 9, and 16, for Migrants, Natives and totals respectively.

First, all those who have a feeling of financial obligations towards parents and brothers did not get the opportunity to fulfil such obligations; not all who got the opportunity fulfilled the obligations. For instance, 96.8% migrant expressed their willingness to fulfil financial obligations towards parents. Of them only 86.8% got the opportunity, and of these about 90% fulfilled the obligation. Almost the same trend exists in the case of (i) native respondents vis-a-vis their parents, (ii) migrant respondents vis-a-vis their brothers, (iii) native respondents vis-a-vis their brothers.

Secondly, compared to the migrants, a smaller proportion of native respondents had a feeling of financial obligation towards both parents and brothers: while 96.8% migrant respondents had a feeling of obligation towards parents, only 64.2% native had this feeling. So far as fulfillment is concerned, native respondents appeared to have fulfilled obligations to a larger degree in comparison to their migrant counterparts. This is an exception to the expected results. But the number of native respondents who got the opportunity to fulfil the obligation and actually fulfilled it is rather small (6).

Thirdly, both migrant and native respondents had less inclination towards giving financial support to brothers in comparison to the same towards parents. The difference was more glaring in the case of native respondents.

Fourthly, only 75% migrant respondents and 42.8% native respondents had this feeling and also fulfilled the financial obligations towards parents. In case of brothers only 37.1% migrant and 14.3% native respondents had the feeling and also fulfilled the financial obligations towards brothers.

Finally, taking migrant and native respondents together, only 73.2% respondents had the feeling and also fulfilled the financial obligations towards parents, and only 34.9% fulfilled obligations towards brothers.

To sum up: the feeling of financial obligations towards parents exists in a greater degree than towards brothers; it implies that while lineal kinship is still very strong, fraternal kinship has considerably weakened. Secondly, the respondents with a rural background have a stronger feeling of financial obligations both towards parents and brothers than those with an urban background. It implies that if migration to the cities increases the feeling of financial obligations towards kith and kin will diminish. This goes in line with our hypothesis. Finally, younger people seem to be less inclined to offer financial support to their kith and kin, particularly when they are living separately.

Non-fulfillment of Financial Obligations Despite Feeling

Among those who reportedly had a feeling of financial obligation towards their parents and brothers, and had an opportunity to offer help, 24 did not do so. It seemed pertinent to find out why this was so. For, mere non-fulfillment of obligations which may be beyond the control of the respondent cannot and should not be taken as indicative of his apathy towards his parents or brothers.

All the respondents not having fulfilled financial obligations despite having got an opportunity to do so belonged to the category of migrants: 16 in case of parents and 8 in case of brothers (Table 4.6, col. 5-7). All the 24 stated their financial inability as the reason for not fulfilling financial obligations. It was difficult to ascertain whether they were really incapable of rendering financial help. However, some possible objective indicators were used to ascertain this. For example, 7 respondents who could not fulfil financial obligations towards their parents/brothers despite their feeling in this regard, had relatively larger families than those who had fulfilled financial obligations. But the remaining 17 had households of a smaller size than those who fulfilled their obligation towards their parents and brothers. This indicates that they were not prepared to cut down on their comforts and spare a part of their resources for the support of their parents and brothers--9 in case of the former and 8 in case of the latter. Therefore, financial inability in their case can hardly be taken as a genuine reason for not fulfilling their financial obligations. One can therefore doubt the genuineness of their feelings, too. If this proposition is granted the number of respondents not having feeling increases to 15--6 having expressed no feeling (Table 4.6, col. 2-3) and 9 against their expressed feelings--in case of parents and to 61--53 having expressed no feeling (Table 4.6, col. 2-3) and 8 against their expressed feeling--in case of brothers, accounting for 7.9% and 46.2% respectively.

Willingness, Unwillingness and Expectations of the Respondents fulfilling Financial Obligations

In our study of jointness between lineally and fraternally related households, our analysis of feeling and fulfillment of financial obligations did not take us far. For, if financial support is not offered or provided spontaneously when the occasion arises or if it is given unwillingly for whatever considerations, it will be erroneous to consider the fulfillment of financial obligations as an adequate indicator of jointness. We, therefore, also studied the conditions under which financial support was provided. While about 91% migrant gave financial help to their parents, only 66.6% native respondents did it willingly. Only a small proportion of respondents gave financial help to their parents unwillingly, i.e., under social compulsion, and with the expectation of return in cash or kind. But here too, the percentage of native respondents is much higher (33.4%) than that of their migrant counterparts (9.22%). Quite surprisingly, most of the respondents, both migrant and native, gave help to their brothers with the expectations of return: a little less than two-thirds of migrant respondents (63.2%) gave financial help to their brothers with the expectation of a return, and all native respondents expected this to be returned from their brothers. Only 25.5% respondents, in all, gave financial help to brothers willingly and without expecting any return.

To sum up: the willingness and expectation pattern in respect of obligations reveals that all those who gave financial help did not do so willingly and without expectation of return. In all, out of 188 respondents whose parents lived separately, only 129 migrant respondents (68.6%) gave financial support to their fathers on different occasions willingly and without expectation. The corresponding percentage for the native respondents was still lower i.e., 28.7%. These facts lead us to the conclusion that jointness between fraternal households of both migrant and native respondents seems to be very weak, as only about one-fourth of the respondents have given financial help willingly and without any expectation of return.

Extent of Help

We have studied the fulfillment of financial obligations as a criteria for judging the jointness of households. The fulfillment of financial obligations, however, cannot be taken as a sufficient criterion of the jointness of households. What is also important is the extent of this financial support and the purpose behind it. Sending an occasional amount of money to one's parents and/or brothers cannot be equated with fulfilling one's financial obligations. We have also to see the spirit in which it is sent. For example, monetary help given with a view to securing one's own interest in landed property can hardly be considered as fulfillment of financial obligations in the real sense of the term. We, therefore, attempted to look also into the purpose and extent of financial help.

No accurate information was available regarding the extent of help provided by the respondents to their parents and brothers. When asked about it, almost all the respondents replied rather evasively by saying that the amount sent by them depended on the nature of the occasion, amount demanded by their relatives, and their own capacity. Some put the amount sent by them between Rs. 50 and Rs. 1000. Since the number of such respondents was very small the extent of help could not be established at all. Except in very few cases, respondents were not certain about the frequency of financial help rendered. They also reported that they had given financial help to parents or brothers on their demand which had rarely been met in full. Most of the respondents reported having sent money out of their current savings. Only six of them reported having borrowed money either from their P.F. or from their friends to help their parents, but none did so in the case of their brothers.

Occasion of Help

The most common occasion of financial support to parents was marriage of younger brothers and sisters. Some of the respondents had an opportunity to help their parents in their medical treatment, but in most cases medical treatment was provided by the Mill, and the respondents bore only the expenditure on the parents' stay with them in the city. Only 9 respondents remitted Rs. 50 to their parents every month. No native respondent reported giving monthly support to his parents.

Thus marriages and medical treatment are the two very common occasions on which respondents selflessly remitted money to their parents but none to their brothers. A few of the respondents sent money to their parents for purposes which involved the existing or expected interest of the respondent, namely, the maintenance of land[2], payment of land revenue, repair or construction of houses. In such cases most of the respondents expressed their eagerness to go back to the villages after their retirement. The financial support extended by this group was motivated by their interest in the landed property owned by their parents. Since the amount sent was only on demand on such occasions as mentioned above, the fulfillment of financial obligations by this group can hardly be considered as a genuine fulfillment of financial obligation. They have been, therefore, excluded from the group of those who have been supporting their parents willingly, selflessly and also without any expectation of return.

Majority of the respondents who had given financial assistance to their brothers had done so on the marriage of their nieces. In most cases the amount spent varied between Rs. 300/- to Rs. 400/- and was mostly in the form of a gift for the bride. Those who had given a substantial amount had done so with the full hope that it would be reciprocated or simply as a loan . Only in two cases did the respondents help their brothers to meet the cost of litigation. None of the respondents had helped their brothers to meet expenses for the cultivation of land where the interest of the respondent was not involved.

Financial Help Sought by the Respondent

We have so far dealt with the respondents' feeling and fulfillment of financial obligations towards parents and brothers. Enquiries were also made to find out whether respondent sought financial help from them in case of need, and whether there was any mutual financial interdependence between the respondent and his related households. So far as migrant are concerned, a majority of them had neither asked their parents nor brothers in their village for financial help, nor did they hope to get any help from them. Some migrant respondents whose parents were in the city expected financial assistance from them in case of need, although such a need had not arisen till then. Almost all the migrant respondents reported that they had a number of sources available in the Mill itself and they hardly needed to look towards anybody else for financial assistance. The Mill provided loans from mutual society and from P.F. Besides, they had a Marriage Fund also from which they could borrow money at the time of marriage of their daughter(s). Only a few depended on other sources, such as borrowings from friends.

From the foregoing analysis one can infer that most of the respondents, migrant or native, are financially independent. Their independence in regard to the fulfillment of their financial requirements may be taken as a cause of weakening of relations between the two households over time. It is only mutual give and take that bring households closer; one way flow of finances weakens the family bonds.

Our findings regarding the feeling and fulfillment of financial obligations can be summed up by grouping the households on the following basis, as in table 4.7.

(i) *Closely related*: In this category are included the households/respondents

(a) having feeling, got opportunity and fulfilled it willingly and without any expectations of return,

(b) having feeling, got no opportunity, but ready to fulfill, and

(c) having feeling, got opportunity, but could not fulfill for genuine reasons.

(ii) *Marginally related*: In this category are included the households/respondents

(a) having feeling, got opportunity and fulfilled unwillingly,

(b) having feeling, got opportunity and fulfilled with a feeling of reciprocation.

(iii) *Nuclear Families*: Respondents who do not have a feeling of financial obligation at all have been placed in this category.

Conclusion

First, lineal jointness in the households has been only very slightly affected by the migration of labour to the city. About 90% of the migrant respondents still fulfill their financial obligations towards their parents willingly and selflessly. A few of them who could not do so had either got no opportunity or had certain genuine reasons for not doing so. These households may be termed as closely related.

Secondly, fraternal jointness seems to have weakened to a large extent, because only 32.6% of the migrant respondents fulfilled their financial obligations towards their brothers' households willingly and without any expectation of return.

Thirdly, in case of native respondents both lineal and fraternal jointness have severely weakened. Only 50% native respondents fulfilled financial obligations towards their parents willingly and selflessly. The corresponding percentage in case of brothers was only 14.2. It seems that in the case of native respondents fraternal jointness has almost disappeared.

Fourthly, our findings also revealed that both lineal and fraternal jointness have grown weaker in the case of native respondents than in the case of migrant. The urban way of life seems to have adversely affected the functional jointness of households so far as fulfillment of financial obligations is concerned.

Thus we found that 87% of the households of our respondents were closely related, 7.4% were marginally related and only the remaining 5.5% were nuclear in relation to their parents. (Table 4.7) The corresponding percentages for fraternal households were about 40, 26 and 43 respectively. The percentage variations indicate that fraternal links are weaker than lineal links. This supports our hypothesis that 'the joint family pattern is expected to be prevalent less in fraternal than in lineal relations'.

TABLE 4.7 : Extent of Jointness between Respondents and their Parents and Brothers on the basis of Feeling and Fulfillment of Financial Obligations by Residential Background

Sr.No.	Extent of Jointness	Migrant		Native		Total	
		Parents	Brothers	Parents	Brothers	Parents	Brothers
1.	Closely related	169 (89.9)	43 (32.6)	7 (50.0)	2 (14.2)	176 (87.1)	45 (30.9)
2.	Marginally related	13 (6.9)	36 (27.3)	2 (14.2)	2 (14.2)	15 (7.4)	38 (26.0)
3.	Nuclear	6 (3.2)	53 (40.1)	5 (35.8)	10 (71.6)	11 (5.5)	63 (43.1)
	Total	188 (100.0)	132 (100.0)	14 (100.0)	14 (100.0)	202 (100.0)	146 (100.0)

(B) Reciprocal Visits

Reciprocal visits is another criterion we chose for judging jointness between households. It is particularly important for the purpose of our study because most of our sample workers had migrated to the city from rural areas. Reciprocal visits--their frequency and purpose--can be taken as a measure of the level of interaction between the households and the degree of filial bondage between the respondents and their affinal households--the households of their parents and/or brothers. This sub-section therefore studies the functional relations between the households on the basis of reciprocal visits by the members of the related households.

Reciprocal visits have been studied from two angles: (i) frequency of visits, and (ii) purpose of visits. Broadly speaking, a high frequency of visits has been taken to indicate a greater degree of jointness. Similarly, reciprocal visits paid with the purpose of meeting parents or brothers and enquiring about their welfare has been taken as a mark of filial bondage and a greater degree of jointness. Reciprocal visits paid infrequently and that too in pursuance of self-interest have been considered as an indicator of weak filial bonds.

The assessment of jointness between households on the basis of the above criterion, however, involved certain problems. The first problem was to ascertain the extent of frequency of visit as an indicator of high or low jointness. One solution to this problem could be to compare the frequency of visits in the recent past with the same in the earlier periods, particularly by the workers of the past generation. But no information in this regard could be gathered from the respondents, nor was any comparable data available for the same set of industrial workers.

Secondly, our respondents varied in regard to the distance between their residence in the city and that of their affinal households. A section of our respondents belonged to Delhi who had their affinal households in the city and others were migrants. Among the migrants, some came from places as distant as Varanasi and Gorakhpur. Therefore, no single criterion could justifiably be applied to all of them. Existing literature on the subject too did not provide any satisfactory solution to this problem.

Thirdly, relating frequency to some time interval, say a week, month, or a year, would not be justified, because time-bound regularity in visits can hardly be maintained. Even an average of visits in these time intervals could not be a reliable index. A respondent may visit his native place four times in a month because of some necessity, such as the illness of some members, but may not otherwise visit at all during one full year. His four visits in a month, therefore, could be taken as a quarterly visit on an average basis.

Finally, any criterion of rating a certain frequency as high or low would remain arbitrary, unless such factors as distance, cost of journey, availability of time, willingness to visit, etc., are not appropriately accounted for. Unfortunately adequate data on this could not be provided by the respondents.

Despite these limitations an attempt was made to study the pattern of reciprocal visits, their frequency and purpose. The reciprocal visits by the migrant and native respondents have been discussed separately because the important factors like time, cost, distance, etc., which affect reciprocal visits are different for the two categories of respondents. After analysing these aspects we have drawn the relevant conclusions with a view to assessing jointness between households on the basis of frequency and purpose of reciprocal visits.

Migrant Respondents

For the purpose of studying reciprocal visits between migrant respondents' nuclear and affinal households, the respondents were divided into different categories, based on the place of location of the affinal households, i.e., city (Delhi), village, or at both the places, and the type of relationship.

As shown in the table (4.8) only 205 out of 247 migrant respondents had their affinal households at their native place. Only this category of respondents would be studied here in regard to reciprocal visits. The remaining 108 respondents having their affinal households in the city would be taken care of in the subsequent subsection which deals with native respondents having their affinal households in the city. Another category of workers (76) is common to both these categories who have been studied in relation to their affinal households in the city and in the village.

TABLE 4.8 : **Distribution of Migrant Respondents by Location of their Affinal Households**

S.No.	Type of relationship	Location of the household		Total
		Native Place	Delhi	
1		2	3	4
1.	Parents	105 +76*	7	188
2.	Brothers	24	76* +32	76* +56
3.	Sons	-	3	3
	Total	205	118	247

* These are the respondents whose parents are at village and brothers in the city. Since they are the same respondents they have been counted only once in the total.

Out of 205 respondents having affinal relatives at the native place 181 [row (1) col. 2 of the table] have been studied in relation to their parental households and 24 [row (3) col. 2 of the table] in relation to their brothers only.

TABLE 4.9 : **Frequency of Visits to Parents and Brothers at the Native Place**

S.No.	Frequency of Visits	Type of Relationship				Total	
		Parents		Brothers			
		No.	%	No.	%	No.	%
1		2	3	4	5	6	7
1.	Monthly	125	69.1	11	45.8	136	66.3
2.	Bi-annually	24	13.2	5	20.8	29	14.2
3.	Annually	20	11.1	4	16.7	24	11.7
4.	Rarely	12	6.6	4	16.7	16	7.8
	Total	181*	100.0	24*	100.0	205	100.0

* Figures taken from Table 4.8

Respondents Visit to Native Place

With a view to knowing the intensity of their relationship with the affinal households at the village, all the respondents were asked whether or not they visited their native place. All of them replied in the affirmative though the frequency of their visit had varied (Table 4.9).

Our enquiry revealed that nearly two-thirds of the respondents (66.3%) were paying monthly visits to their native place. Keeping in view the nature of their job, and the busy life in a metropolitan city like Delhi, it can be said that jointness in these cases exists in the highest degree. These respondents may be said to be very much attached to their affinal households and may, therefore, be considered closely related with them.

Slightly more than one-fourth (25.9%) of the respondents reported paying bi-annual or annual visits: 14.2% bi-annually, and the remaining 11.7% annually. If one considers the proportion of the migrant respondents living within the radius of 60 kms. (on an average) from Delhi, annual or even bi-annual visits appear to be a very low frequency of visits: such a low frequency could be justified in the case of respondents who came from far off places like Varanasi and Gorakhpur in U.P., and Jaipur and Ajmer in Rajasthan, but not in the case of those who came from the adjoining areas. The remaining 8% of the respondents reported visiting their native place rarely. But given the distance, cost of travelling in terms of both money and time, lack of holidays and week-long tiring work, bi-annual visits may be considered neither a high nor a low frequency of visits. The frequency of visits, however, did not furnish any conclusive evidence regarding the nature and extent of jointness between the respondents and the affinal households in the native place. Nevertheless, it can safely be said that quite a sizeable number of the respondents maintain relations with their affinal households. But the closeness between lineal relatives seems to be greater than between fraternal relatives. A comparison between the frequency of visits paid to parents and brothers (cols. 3 and 5) proves the point. While 69.1% of the respondents paid monthly visits to their parents, only 45.8% visited their brothers. This can be taken as an indicator of closer bonds between the lineal relatives than between the fraternal ones, and as a confirmatory test of the trend that has already been marked with regard to the feeling and fulfillment of financial obligations, our first criterion.

Purpose of Visit

As already pointed out the frequency of visits is not a sufficient indicator of the extent of jointness between the respondents and their affinal households at the native place. To assess jointness, we have further considered the respondents' purpose of visit to his native place on the following basis:

i. Respondents visiting their parents/brothers out of affection and good will have been considered *closely related* with their affinal households. This category also includes those who combine their visit with the celebration of festivals and ceremonies.
ii. Respondents visiting only on the occasions of deaths or marriages have been considered only *marginally related*.
iii. Those visiting essentially in their own interest have been categorised as belonging to *nuclear families*.

Most of the respondents reported more than one purpose of their visits. For reasons of exactness and accuracy we took into consideration only the purpose that was given top priority by them. Purpose-wise responses have been presented in table 4.10.

TABLE 4.10 : **Respondents Purpose of Visit to Their Parents and Brothers at Native Place**

S.No.	Purpose of Visit	Type of Relationship				Total	
		Parents		Brothers			
		No.	%	No.	%	No.	%
	1	2	3	4	5	6	7
1.	Wife and/or children at village	19	10.5	-	-	19	9.2
2.	Participation in festivals and ceremonies and meeting relations.	106	58.5	11	45.8	117	57.1
3.	When necessary (Death, marriage etc.)	44	24.4	9	37.5	53	25.9
4.	Keeping claim alive	12	6.6	-	-	12	5.9
5.	Claiming share	-	-	4	16.7	4	1.9
	Total	181	100.0	24	100.0	205	100.0

The table shows that the majority of the respondents (57.1%) visited their parents and brothers for: (i) taking part in festivals and participating in marriage ceremonies, (ii) knowing their welfare, and (iii) helping them in the celebration of marriage and other ceremonies, etc. Since the respondents of this category appeared to have a sense of concern towards their affinal relatives, and, reportedly, paid regular visits without any apparent selfish motive, they have been considered closely related to their affinal relatives. Respondents visiting to meet their wives and children (9.2%) have also been included in this category for the simple reason that these respondents had left the members of their nuclear units--wives and children--under the care of their (respondents') parents and were putting up with them. This in itself was indicative of the fact that relations of these respondents with their parents were very cordial. All such respondents had left their wives and children at the native place willingly. Their inclusion in the first category of respondents pushes the percentage of closely related households to nearly two-thirds (66.3%) of the total.

About one-fourth (25.9%) of the respondents reported that they paid visits only when they became necessary. They visited their native place on such occasions as death or marriage ceremony, disputes, repeated insistence of parents/brothers or their ill health. Their visit seemed to be prompted more by social compulsion than by their sweet will. Respondents of this category did not seem to be as eager to maintain relations through frequent visits to their affinal relatives as the respondents placed in the first category. They have been, therefore, categorised as marginally related households. The remaining respondents (about 8%) have straightaway been designated as nuclear households as they did not hesitate to mention that the main purpose of their visit was to secure their own interest -- to keep their claim in ancestral property alive, and to claim their share in the produce from land. Explaining their rare visits, most of them pointed out that their grown up children were apathetic towards rural life and discouraged them to pay visits to their native place. They wanted to celebrate festivals in the city with greater fanfare. Also, their children prevented them from investing any money in the native place. A few of the respondents visited rarely because their relations with parents were uncordial. They apprehended that their not visiting the native place would deprive them of their claims on the ancestral property. Two of the four respondents visiting their brothers to claim their share had given land to non-relatives as their sharecroppers. All the four visited their native place only to claim their share in the produce.

Applying the criterion on the same lines, a comparison of the percentage figures in col 3 and 5 (Table 4.10) clearly brings out variations in the extent of jointness between (i) respondents' and their parents, and (ii) respondents and their brothers. As many as 69% (58.5% + 10.5%) respondents are closely related to their parents, while only 45.8% respondents are closely related to brothers, indicating a closer bond between lineal groups than fraternal groups. This is further supported by the fact that as the degree of jointness decreases, the percentage of respondents in the category of marginally related and nuclear household increases. While only 24.4% respondents are marginally related with their parents and only 6.6% are nuclear, the corresponding percentages for brothers are 37.5 and 16.7 respectively. Our findings help us to conclude that jointness between fraternally related households has weakened considerably.

Relations Visiting the Respondent : Reciprocity

We have analysed above the pattern of respondents' frequency and purpose of visits to their native place. Since relations depend on reciprocity, this sub-section is devoted to the study of return-visits paid, if any, by the parents and brothers of the respondents and also the purpose of their visits. Our purpose here is to find out (i) whether or not the respondents' relatives visit them, and (ii) whether respondents invite their affinal relatives--parents and brothers. Those expressing reluctance towards inviting their relations were asked to give the reasons for this. An enquiry was also made regarding the purpose of their visit.

Most of the 181 respondents whose parents were at village had reportedly invited them to the city but their parents had visited them only infrequently or rarely because they were mostly busy with their work in the native place. Parents who visited the respondents usually did so for receiving medical treatment and, in certain cases, on national occasions such as 15th August or 26th January. Respondents whose parents were not doing anything particular at the village could not invite them for permanent stay for lack of proper accommodation and costly urban living. The helplessness of the respondents in this case was understandable. Only two respondents frankly confessed that they had not invited their parents to stay with them because of uncordial relations. They apprehended that their visit would aggravate tension between their parents and their wives.

Surprisingly, none of the respondents reported having invited his brother to stay with him. Only four migrant respondents had brought younger brothers to their place for giving them proper education, since adequate educational facilities were not available at their native place. No respondent was found having shown a similar favour to his nephew, though many had nephews. Our enquiry also revealed that none of the respondents was ready to keep his brother with him permanently. In 13 cases, brothers no doubt visited the respondents, but in many cases either for receiving better medical facilities or for getting a job in the city.

To sum up, respondents' relatives reciprocated visits rarely, that too, mainly for medical treatment or for searching a job in the city. Where parents were invited, they did not respond either because they had their own engagements at the village or because they did not like to be a burden on their children in a costly city like Delhi. Visits by brothers were rare because they were only rarely invited. Those who visited without being invited, did so under force of circumstances, such as illness and unemployment. This again is as indication of the weakening fraternal links.

Respondents' Relatives in Delhi

After studying the pattern of reciprocal visits between the migrant respondents and their relations at village, we now examine the pattern of reciprocal visits between (i) migrant respondents and their relatives, and (ii) native respondents and their relatives, both in the city. A section of migrant respondents and all the native respondents had affinal households in the city. Most of the respondents reported having one or more relatives in the city. In our study, however, we have considered only those respondents who have parents and/or brothers living in a separate household in the city.

TABLE 4.11 : **Respondents Whose Parents and Brothers are living separately in Delhi by Residential Background**

S.No.	Type of Relationship	Residential background				Total	
		Migrant		Native			
		No.	%	No.	%	No.	%
	1	2	3	4	5	6	7
1.	Parents	7	6.2	14	50.0	21	14.8
2.	Brothers	108	93.8	14	50.0	122	85.2
	Total	115*	100.0	28@	100.0	143	100.0

* This figure does not include 3 respondents in whose case only sons were living separately.

@ This figure does not include 7 respondents in whose case sons were living separately.

Table 4.11 presents the distribution of migrant and native respondents having their parents, and/or brother(s) living separately in Delhi. Out of 282 respondents (247 migrant and 35 native) living in nuclear households, only 143 (115 migrant and 28 native) had either parents or brothers in the city. Ten respondents (3 migrant and 7 native) having only son(s) in separate households were however ignored because of their negligible number in the former category in proportion to the total number. It is evident from the table that parents of only 14.8% respondents lived separately while as many as 85.2% reported that their brothers lived in a separate household. In order to assess the extent of jointness between the respondents and their affinal households in the city we adopted the same method as in the case of migrant and their relations at village.

Frequency of Visits

For studying the frequency of visits, we grouped the meetings between the respondents and their relatives in six categories (Table 4.12). The first three are visits at regular time intervals, viz., weekly, fortnightly, and monthly. The fourth one is occasional i.e., meeting only on the occasion of festivals and ceremonies. The remaining two categories show rare or no meetings. Accordingly, we formulated

TABLE 4.12 : **Frequency of meetings between Respondents and their Parents and Brothers in the City by Residential Background**

Sr. No.	Frequency of meetings	Type of Relationship						Total		
		PARENTS			BROTHERS					
		Residential Background			Residential Background					
		Migrant	Native	Total	Migrant	Native	Total	Migrant	Native	Total
1.	Weekly	1 (14.2)	1 (7.1)	2 (9.5)	7 (6.4)	2 (14.4)	9 (7.3)	8 (6.9)	3 (10.7)	11 (7.7)
2.	Fortnightly	- (-)	4 (28.7)	4 (19.0)	29 (26.8)	4 (28.5)	33 (27.1)	29 (25.2)	8 (28.5)	37 (25.9)
3.	Monthly	2 (28.6)	4 (28.7)	6 (28.5)	41 (38.0)	- (-)	41 (33.6)	43 (37.4)	4 (14.3)	47 (32.9)
	Total 1 + 2 + 3	3 (42.8)	9 (64.5)	12 (57.0)	77 (71.2)	6 (42.9)	83 (68.0)	80 (69.5)	15 (53.5)	95 (66.5)
4.	Festivals and ceremonies	2 (28.6)	2 (14.2)	4 (19.0)	11 (10.2)	3 (21.4)	14 (11.5)	13 (11.4)	5 (17.8)	18 (12.5)
5.	Rarely*	2 (28.6)	1 (7.1)	3 (14.5)	12 (11.2)	5 (35.7)	17 (14.0)	14 (12.2)	6 (21.5)	20 (14.0)
6.	Never	- (-)	2 (14.2)	2 (9.5)	8 (7.4)	- (-)	8 (6.5)	8 (6.9)	2 (7.2)	10 (7.0)
	Total 5 + 6	2 (28.6)	3 (21.3)	5 (24.0)	20 (18.6)	5 (35.7)	25 (20.5)	22 (19.1)	8 (28.7)	30 (21.0)
	Grand Total (1 to 6)	7 (100.0)	14 (100.0)	21 (100.0)	108 (100.0)	14 (100.0)	122 (100.0)	115 (100.0)	28 (100.0)	143 (100.0)

* One in 3 or 4 years time.

three criteria to judge the degree of jointness between households on the basis of the frequency of their meetings.

(i) Meetings at regular time intervals, such as weekly, fortnightly or monthly, as social calls have been taken as an index of high degree of jointness. Such households have, therefore, been placed in the category of *closely related* households.

(ii) Meeting relations living in the same city only on the occasion of festivals and family ceremonies has been taken to indicate a low degree of jointness: these households have been considered *marginally related*.

(iii) No or rare meetings have been taken as an indicator of lack of jointness between households; such households have been considered as *nuclear*.

The over-all picture of the extent of jointness on the basis of reciprocal visits or meetings betwee the respondents and their affinal relatives--both parents and br aers--is tabulated in table 4.12. It shows that majority of the respondents (66.5%) are closely related with their affinal relatives. Of the remaining 33.5%, about 13% are marginally related, the rest are nuclear. In spite of the existence of over-all jointness, variations on the basis of residential background and the type of relationships are quite evident and have been elaborately analysed below.

Columns 2,3, and 4 (Table 4.12) give us an idea about the extent of jointness that exists between the respondents and their parents. In all, the parents of 21 respondents (7 migrant and 14 native) lived separately in the city. Relations were cordial only in the case of 12 respondents (57%) where meetings between respondents and their parents took place either weekly, fortnightly, or monthly. Only these respondents can be considered closely related with their parents. Of the remaining 9 respondents relations of 4 are relatively less cordial because they met their parents only on festivals and ceremonies. They have been considered marginally related to their parental households. Meetings in 3 of the remaining 5 cases took place rarely i.e., only during emergencies. The remaining 2 reported that no meetings had taken place between them and their parents after they had separated three or four years before. A detailed interview with those two respondents revealed that their in-laws were also in Delhi and in time of need they took their (in-law's) help. These two respondents did not only have a nuclear household but a nuclear family as well. The three respondents who have had rare meetings with their parents have also been included in this category.

A comparison between migrant and native respondents shows that jointness between native households seems to be greater than in the case of migrant households. Against 64.5% native households, only 42.8% migrant households were found to be closely related to parents. A similar pattern exists in regard to marginally related and nuclear families.

Assessing the nature of relations between respondents and their brothers by applying the same criteria, cordiality existed only in 83 cases (68%) where meetings took place weekly, fortnightly or monthly in case of 9, 33 and 41 respondents respectively. Of the remaining 39 cases (32%), 8 reported not having met their brothers at all after separation, because separation in these cases had taken place in very uncongenial circumstances. Meetings in 17 cases had been rare. The remaining 14 respondents reported meeting their brothers only on festivals and ceremonies. To conclude, in the case of the fraternal households 68% are closely related, 11.5% are marginally related, while 21% are nuclear.

The break-up of respondents on the basis of residential background reveal that while in the case of migrants relations are cordial in more than 70% cases, the corresponding percentage among the native is only 43. Those having comparatively less cordial relations and meeting only on festivals and ceremonies are more amongst the native (21.4%) than amongst the migrants (10.2%). The households which may be said to be nuclear in relation to their fraternal households are 35.7% among the native and only 18.6% among the migrants.

Thus, judged on the basis of reciprocal visits, familial bonds between lineally related households seem to be much stronger in case of native respondents than in the case of migrants. Conversely familial bonds between fraternally related households appear to be stronger in the case of migrants.

Purpose of Meeting

Purpose of visit is an equally important aspect of reciprocal visits because it gives an idea about the intention behind meetings. The final assessment was, however, made on the basis of both frequency and purpose of meetings. Assessment of jointness on the basis of purpose of meeting has been done on the following lines:

i. Respondents and their affinal relatives calling on each other purely for the purpose of seeing each other have been considered *closely related.*

ii. Those meeting only on festivals and ceremonies have been taken as *marginally related.*

iii. Those meeting only on the occasion of emergency or not having met at all after separation have been considered as *nuclear.*

As many as 71.4% respondents visited each other for seeing each other (Table 4.13). Since meetings were usually without any selfish motive, and the frequency of meetings was weekly, fortnightly or monthly, they have been considered closely related (Table 4.12).

Those meeting only on festivals and ceremonies are 18 in number and account for 13.6%. This number is corroborated even by table 4.12. Given the fact that (i) our respondents are Hindus, and (ii) there are at least three important Hindu festivals, (viz., Holi, Diwali, Dushehra) on which meeting relations (if not otherwise indisposed) is almost obligatory, it can be safely inferred that the respondents of this category and their relations must be meeting thrice a year. For the people living in the same city, meeting relations only thrice a year, that too, only as a social obligation, is certainly a low frequency. These households have, therefore, been considered only marginally related.

TABLE 4.13 · **Purpose of Meetings between Respondents and their Parents and Brothers in the City by their Residential Background**

Sr. No.	Purpose of Meeting	Type of Relationship: Parents — Residential Background			Type of Relationship: Brothers — Residential Background			Total		
		Migrant	Native	Total	Migrant	Native	Total	Migrant	Native	Total
	1	2	3	4	5	6	7	8	9	10
1.	Social call	3 (42.8)	9 (75.0)	12 (63.1)	77 (77.0)	6 (42.8)	83 (72.8)	80 (74.8)	15 (57.7)	95 (71.4)
2.	Festivals and ceremonies	2 (28.6)	2 (16.6)	4 (21.5)	11 (11.0)	3 (21.4)	14 (12.4)	13 (12.2)	5 (19.3)	18 (13.6)
3.	Emergency	2 (28.6)	1 (8.4)	3 (15.4)	12 (12.0)	5 (35.8)	17 (14.8)	14 (13.0)	6 (23.0)	20 (15.0)
	Total	7 (100.0)	12 (100.0)	19 (100.0)	100 (100.0)	14 (100.0)	114 (100.0)	107 (100.0)	26 (100.0)	133* (100.0)

* This figure does not include 10 respondents in whose case no meeting has taken place after separation.

Meetings in the case of the remaining 20 respondents (15%) took place only because of some unpleasant or pleasant emergency, such as illness, death, marriage. Such households have, therefore, been treated as nuclear families. Inclusion of ten respondents who had not met after a split pushes the percentage of such respondents to 21 (col. 10 Table 4.12). All of them have been considered as nuclear families.

Applying the same criterion for making a comparison between native and migrant respondents the jointness between native households is weaker than between migrant households: only about 58% native respondents seem to be closely related with their affinal households against the corresponding percentage of about 75 for the migrant respondents. Marginally related and nuclear households among the migrant are only 12.2 and 13.0% respectively, against the corresponding percentages of 19.3 and 23.0 in the case of native households.

The trend with regard to fraternal relations is in consonance with the over-all trend on the basis of residential background: among the migrants closely related, marginally related, and nuclear households are 77.0%, 11.0% and 12.0% respectively, while in the case of native, the corresponding percentages are 42.8, 21.4 and 35.8. Quite unexpectedly, about 75% native respondents are closely related to their parents as compared to only 42.8% migrant respondents of this category. Only 16.5% native respondents are marginally related; the corresponding percentage for the migrant is 28.6. Against 8.4% native respondents having nuclear households, 28.6% migrant are living in nuclear households.

Conclusion

In studying the extent of jointness between the respondents and their affinal households on the basis of frequency and purpose of visits, our major findings in table 4.14 are:

First, over-all jointness existed in a large measure in case of both lineally and fraternally related households. About 68% respondents' households including both migrant and native were closely related with their parental household and about 65% were closely related to

TABLE 4.14 : **Extent of Jointness between Respondents and Their Parents and Brothers on the Basis of Reciprocal Visits by Residential Background**

S. No.	Extent of Jointness	Residential Background: Migrants, Type of Relationship: Parents			Brothers			Native, Type of Relationship		Total, Type of Relationship	
		In Village	In city	Total	In city	In village	Total	Parents	Brothers	Parents	Brothers
	1	2	3	4	5	6	7	8	9	10	11
1.	Closely related	125	3	128 (68.0)	77	11	88 (66.2)	9 (64.2)	6 (42.8)	137 (67.8)	94 (64.3)
2.	Marginally related	44	2	46 (24.5)	11	9	20 (15.2)	2 (14.3)	3 (21.4)	48 (23.7)	23 (15.7)
3.	Nuclear	12	2	14 (7.5)	20	4	24 (18.2)	3 (21.5)	5 (35.8)	17 (8.5)	29 (20.0)
	Total	181	7	188 (100.0)	108	24	132 (100.0)	14 (100.0)	14 (100.0)	202 (100.0)	146 (100.0)

Sources for:
Col. 2, col. 2, table 4.10
Col. 3, col. 2, table 4.12
Col. 5, col. 5, table 4.12
Col. 6, col. 4, table 4.10
Col. 8, col. 3, table 4.12
Col. 9, col. 6, table 4.12

the households of their brothers. Also, one-fifth of the households are nuclear in relation to brothers though only 8.5% are nuclear in relation to parents.

Secondly, there are variations in accordance with the residential background in spite of over-all jointness. Among the migrants (col. 4 and 7) 68% were closely related to their parental households and 66.2% to brothers, whereas, among the native (col. 8 and 9), only about 64% and 43% are closely related to their parents and brothers respectively.

Finally, jointness between lineally related households exists in a larger measure than between fraternally related households, in case of both migrant and native households, though the difference is wider in case of the latter. Similarly, nucleation of households is greater among native respondents than among the migrants.

(C) Seeking Advice and Approval of Elders[3]

The third criterion that we have chosen for finding out the extent of jointness between the respondents' and their affinal households is 'seeking advice and approval of elders' by the respondents on issues like purchase of land, settling marriage of children, schooling of children, and celebration of ceremonies like 'mundan' etc.

This criterion is important because in the traditional family system 'age' was very much respected; all issues, major or minor, were normally decided by the eldest male member of a family. His authority was unchallengeable and his decisions final:"...age was generally an important element governing social status and privilege in extended families" (Yogendra Singh, 1973: 174). The head of family could, however, exercise his authority over the members of the extended family only when such families lived within a close proximity of his residence. But in the case of extended families which are widely dispersed such a direct exercise of authority would be difficult. Under these conditions, the exercise of the authority by the head can be envisaged only through postal communication or through sending of messages, though it poses difficulties of its own. However, the effectiveness of the authority of the head of a family can be ascertained by finding out whether heads of nuclear units--the respondents--seek permission or advice of the head--father or elder brother--on such important matters as settling and organising children's marriage, buying of property, or other family ceremonies such as 'mundan' and 'yagyopavit'. In case they do so we can say that such units are extensions of a joint family.

Keeping in view this hypothesis, we proceeded to study the operative part of the elder's authority on the households of the industrial worker, assuming that the worker's nuclear household was a mere extension of a joint family. We have in this sub-section tried to test this hypothesis by finding out the extent of jointness between the respondents' and other affinal households on the basis of their responses under the following three categories.

(i) Complete dependence on the advice and approval of elders has been taken as indicative of complete integration between the affinal households and such cases have been considered as *closely related*;
(ii) those reporting partial dependence have been classified as *marginally related*; and
(iii) those who did not seek advice and approval of their elders have been considered as having *nuclear families*.

This aspect of functional relationship could not be applied to all the respondents because some of them had no living parents nor elder brothers. Enquiries regarding this aspect were, therefore, specifically made only from those respondents who had either their parents alive, or in their absence, had their elder brothers not living with them. Out of 282 nuclear households, only 255 belonged to this category, including 22 native and 233 migrant households. Their responses have been presented in table 4.15.

Native Respondents

Out of 22 respondents on whom this criterion could be applied only 14 had their parents alive. Two out of these (14.3%) reported their complete dependence on the advice and approval of parents in respect of major as well as minor issues. Both the respondents had separated from their parents due to inadequate accommodation. Only these two respondents seemed to be very much attached to the

TABLE 4.15 : **Extent of Respondents' Dependence on the Advice and Approval of Elders by Residential Background**

Sr. No.	Extent of dependence	Residential Background						Total		
		Native			Migrant					
		Type of Relationship			Type of Relationship			Type of Relationship		
		Parents	Brothers	Total	Parents	Brothers	Total	Parents	Brothers	Total
	1	2	3	4	5	6	7	8	9	10
1.	Completely	2 (14.3)	1 (12.5)	3 (13.7)	83 (44.1)	9 (20.0)	92 (39.4)	85 (42.0)	10 (18.9)	95 (37.2)
2.	Partially	7 (50.0)	3 (37.5)	10 (45.4)	99 (52.6)	12 (26.6)	111 (47.6)	106 (52.4)	15 (28.3)	121 (47.4)
3.	Not at all	5 (35.7)	4 (50.0)	9 (40.9)	6 (3.3)	24 (53.4)	30 (13.0)	11 (5.6)	28 (52.8)	39 (15.4)
	Total	14	8*	22	188	45@	233	202	53	255

* Out of 14 respondents not having parents alive, only 8 had elder brothers

@ Only 45 migrant respondents have elder brothers living separately and the parents are not alive.

traditional norms of behaviour. They felt that parents should always be given due recognition for their rich and ripe experience, and as tradition demanded, they were to be given full authority to decide everything about the family affairs, even though the sons lived separately. These two households could be regarded as completely integrated with the parent family, and, therefore, could be considered as closely related. Of the remaining ones, 7 respondents (50%) reported that they would definitely seek the advice of parents on very important issues like children's marriage but they were neither always dependent on it nor did they consider it always obligatory to act according to parental advice. Their seeking advice of parents was, therefore, perfunctory. Incidentally, these respondents had separated from their parents in unpleasant circumstances but their relations with them had improved over time. Such households could, therefore, be considered only marginally joint. The remaining 5 respondents (35.7%) (four having separated from their parents as a result of clashes, and one on the insistence of his wife) reported that till then they had never consulted their parents on any issue. The nuclear households of these respondents could therefore be regarded as nuclear families.

So far as fraternal jointness is concerned, only one out of 8 respondents reported his full dependence on his brother's advice and approval on almost all the major or minor decisions he would take. He had separated from his brother because of inadequate accommodation. Of the remaining 7 respondents, 3 (37.5%) reported that they sought advice of their elder brothers as a matter of courtesy; only to get an opinion and did not feel bound to accept it. In their case consultation or seeking advice was perfunctory, since the only feeling they had was to keep the elder brothers informed of the significant decision taken by them. The remaining 4 (50%) respondents neither consulted nor depended on the advice of their brothers. They felt that elders were out to exploit the young ones.

The figures relating to the total respondents in relation to lineal and fraternal households reveal that only in about 14% cases, there is complete dependence on the elders' advice and approval, and the households are closely related, having a high degree of jointness. For 45.4% native respondents consultation or seeking advice is only perfunctory in nature; making their households only marginally related.

The households of the remaining 40.9% respondents were not only nuclear households but nuclear families as well.

Another significant conclusion which can be drawn from table 4.15 is that there seems to be a greater degree of jointness between the respondents and their lineal households than that between respondents' fraternal households. While about 64% respondents are either fully or partially dependent on their parents for their advice and approval on matters of importance, only 50% respondents consulted their elder brothers. Similarly, the households termed as independent of their lineal households, so far as seeking advice and approval is concerned, accounted for only about 36.0% of the total native respondents, whereas the corresponding percentage was 50.0 in the case of brothers.

The Migrant Respondents

Out of 247 migrant respondents in nuclear households, only 188 had their parents alive and only 45 had elder brothers. Therefore, only 188 respondents could be studied in relation to parents and 45 in relation to elder brothers so far as seeking advice and approval of elders is concerned. The responses in this regard are tabulated in table 4.15.

In all 44.1% reported getting parental advice and approval as an indispensable part of their household functioning. Majority of them reported that they had always tried to celebrate major ceremonies completely in accordance with the wishes of their parents and they could never think of doing anything without parental approval. A few of them however pointed out that they did not want to go against the wishes of parents, especially the father, as this might deprive them of their share, wholly or partially, in their parent's property. These households, though separate are fully integrated with the parent family. More than half of the respondents (52.6%) reported that they had all respect and regard for their parents, but it was not always possible to work according to their wishes. They gave two reasons for this: (i) it was difficult to seek the approval and advice of parents on all issues because of long distance, and (ii) it was not always possible to go by the advice of their parents because it would very often clash with the wishes of their grown-up children who had been brought up in a different environment, and they could not ignore them. These respondents did not occasionally consult their parents, but rarely acted on their advice, since it rarely conformed with the respondents' environment. The remaining 6 (3.3%) had severed relations with their parents. These six households could therefore be regarded nuclear families as well. One interesting fact that the investigation revealed was that though the parents of 7 lived in the city they hardly maintained any relations with them.

The total number of migrant respondents studied in relation to their elder brothers was 45. Of them 24 had elder brothers in the native place and 21 had brothers in the city. A comparison between col. 5 and 6 (Table 4.15) clearly shows that in native as well as migrant respondents the fraternal links were much weaker than the lineal ones so far as consultation and seeking advice on the matters of importance was concerned. Only 20% migrant respondents reported full dependence on their elder brothers compared to 44.1% in the case of parents. They also reported that after their parents, they considered their elder brothers as head of the family, and sought their advice and acted according to their instructions. To the second category belong the respondents (26.6%) who do seek elder brothers' advice but act according to their own wishes. In their case seeking advice is a matter of formality; actually, they want only to keep their brothers informed of their actions. The majority (53.4%) of the respondents reported that they neither sought the advice of their brothers nor asked for their approval. They mentioned that since they had separated due to clashes between them, there was no point in consulting them. This percentage (3.3) is far much higher than the corresponding percentage in the case of parents.

Table 4.15 also reveals that only 39.4% migrant respondents in relation to parents and brothers are closely related with their affinal households so far as seeking advice and approval of elders is concerned. Nearly half (47.6%) of the respondents are only partially dependent, whatever the reasons, and can, therefore, be considered only marginally related. The remaining 13% are not only nuclear households but nuclear families as well.

Conclusion

From the foregoing discussion, the following major conclusions can be drawn. First, native respondents reveal a lower tendency of being dependent on their elders for taking decisions on their affairs than their migrant counterparts. About 41% households of native respondents have assumed characteristics of nuclear family in respect of seeking advice and approval of elders, whereas the corresponding percentage for their migrant counterpart is only 13.0. Besides, while in this regard, only 14% native respondents seem to be closely related with their lineal and fraternal households, a little more than 39% of migrant households are closely related. Secondly, there seems to be a lower degree of affinity between fraternal households in case of both native and migrant respondents in comparison to the lineal households. While 42.0% of respondents (both native and migrant) have expressed their dependence on their parental households with regard to seeking advice and approval, only about 20.0% are dependent on fraternal households. Finally and more significantly, quite a substantial percentage of households-45.4% native and 47.6 migrant respondents--considered as marginally related seem to be in the process of nucleation, since their dependence on the elders for their advice and approval is showing a downward trend.

(D) Exchange/Rendering of Personal Services

We have so far dealt with three criteria--feeling and fulfillment of financial obligations, reciprocal visits, and seeking of advice and approval of elders by the respondents--for assessing the extent of jointness between the respondent and his affinal households. Another important criterion that we adopted in this regard is exchange of personal services between the respondents and other affinal households of migrant and native respondents, living in village and/or city.

The adoption of this criterion is based on the hypothesis that the traditional joint family functioned as a provider of social security. Members within the family in need of physical services at the time of marriage ceremonies, illness, delivery etc. could easily depend on other members of the joint family. It worked on the principle: 'All for each and each for all'. The members of the joint family lived together under one roof; even when they lived separately, small joint families or nuclear units lived in close proximity, generally having one common compound, they were easily approachable by each other during times of need. This tradition of coming to each other's rescue was rooted in social tradition. Failure in fulfilling these obligations was condemned by the village folk and no individual within family would like to incur the displeasure of the village people.

Feeling of oneness and a sense of responsibility to help each other in case of need had served as a family security and a basis for the sustenance of the joint family. But of late, the State has provided an alternative to the personal services rendered by the members of a family to each other. Hospital facility by the State and other medical benefits are some instances of alternative services provided by the society as a substitute for personal services. Besides, in cities and towns some private agencies also provide similar services like catering and other services on the occasion of marriage etc. But such services cannot be expected to be availed by the poorer sections of our society, including the industrial workers. Therefore, such people rely still on the services and help of their kith and kin. But in cases of delivery and illness, they do get hospitalisation facilities subsidized by their employer.

The availability of extra familial facilities as alternatives to the personal services exchanged between the members of a family may be supposed to have reduced the dependence of respondents on their relations, at least for two reasons: (i) high cost and longer time involved in availing the services of relations living at distant places, and (ii) non availability of the services of relatives on full time basis away from residence. Our endeavour in this section is to find out whether such a change has taken place in case of industrial workers, i.e., whether respondents expect and rely on the services of their kith and kin--parents and brothers--and also whether they are prepared to reciprocate. To find the degree of jointness in respect of mutual exchange of personal services, we used the following basis:

(i) Households whose respondents expressed their willingness to render personal services in future and have done so (even if rarely) in the past have been taken to be *closely related*. Respondents willing to do so, though having got no opportunity to do so have also been included in this category.

(ii) Where respondents were willing to give and take personal services, but were not doing so, for certain reasons, their households have been considered *marginally related*; and

(iii) Households belonging to such respondents as had neither exchanged personal services nor were willing to do so in future have been considered as *nuclear families*.

A few points in regard to the analysis which follows need mention here. Since the respondents reported that they have had rare occasions--once in three or four years--to render or to receive personal services, we have studied this aspect mainly in regard to their willingness to exchange personal services. Further, we found during our enquiry that respondents did not discriminate between various occasions when personal services were expected or rendered. They reportedly treated occasions like marriage, illness, delivery as equally important in regard to rendering or exchanging personal services. We have not, therefore, made any distinction between occasions and have straightaway studied the respondents' attitude on the basis of (i) their residential background (i.e., native and migrant), and (ii) their related affinal households (parents and brothers). These responses are presented in table 4.16.

Native Respondents

The table shows that 10 out of 14 respondents (71.6%) reported that they would readily render personal services to their parents, and all of them had done so in the past. Two respondents (14.2%) had not got any opportunity to render services but categorically stated that they would happily serve their parents in case of need. If the respondents of the latter category are taken at their word, the percentage of those who are ready to render personal services unhesitatingly and readily rises to 85.8%. When asked whether they expected same services from parents, they replied in the positive. In most cases, where the need had arisen, parents were reported to have offered their services more readily. Some of the respondents in this category had earlier reported lack of feeling of financial obligations towards parents. And when they were asked to give reasons for

TABLE 4.16 : **Exchange/Rendering of Personal Services between Respondents and Their Parents and Brothers by Residential Background**

Sr. No.	Nature of exchanging personal services	Residential			Background			Total		
		Native			Migrant					
		Type of relationship			Type of relationship			Type of relationship		
		Parents	Brothers	Total	Parents	Brothers	Total	Parents	Brothers	Total
	1	2	3	4	5	6	7	8	9	10
1	Willing and exchanging	10 (71.6)	9 (64.5)	19 (67.8)	153 (80.3)	78 (59.1)	231 (72.3)	163 (80.6)	87 (59.6)	250 (71.8)
2	Willing but no opportunity	2 (14.2)	2 (14.2)	4 (14.3)	32 (17.0)	22 (16.7)	54 (16.8)	34 (16.9)	24 (16.4)	58 (16.7)
3	Willing but not exchanging	1 (7.1)	2 (14.2)	3 (10.8)	- (-)	21 (15.9)	21 (6.6)	1 (0.5)	23 (15.8)	24 (6.8)
4	Neither willing nor exchanging	1 (7.1)	1 (7.1)	2 (7.1)	3 (2.7)	11 (8.3)	14 (4.3)	4 (2.9)	12 (8.20)	16 (4.7)
	Total	14*	14@	28	188**	132@@	320	202	146	348

* Do not have brothers.
@ Do not have parents alive.
** Respondents having separated from parents (alive)
@@ Including 76 respondents having separated from both parents and brothers.

the difference in response to the two situations, they reported that financial obligations involved number of considerations, such as the willingness of wife, one's own responsibilities (children), and the causes of separation. But they mentioned that parents were parents, and even if one could not help them financially, it was a moral, social and religious obligation to take care of them. In the remaining two cases, one reported his willingness to serve his parents in case of need, but could not do so for non-availability of long leave and also because his parents lived far away from his place. A solitary respondent expressed his complete indifference towards mutual exchange of services in case of need, mainly because he had a grouse against his parents; we have treated it as an exception.

On the whole a vast majority of native respondents can be said to be closely related to their lineal households on the basis of services actually rendered or their readiness to offer services in case the need arose. The two cases where respondents did not get an opportunity to do so make no significant difference in our conclusion.

As in the case of lineal relatives, the majority of respondents (64.5%) reported their readiness to render personal services to fraternal relatives in case of any eventuality, though a few of the respondents of this category had separated from their brothers in very unpleasant circumstances, and had refused to render personal services. Only two respondents, (14.2%) who got no occasion to offer their services, expressed their willingness to offer their services to their brothers, whenever called for, in spite of uncordial relations[4]. The aggregate of the respondents, who had done so and those who were ready to do so account for more than three-fourths (78.7%) of the total native respondents. Two respondents (14.2%) though willing to render personal services did not do so because they had clashed with their relatives. This proves that the majority of households of respondents are closely related to their fraternal households.

However, a comparative study of percentage figures in cols. 2 and 3 (Table 4.16) indicates that respondents were more readily prepared to offer personal services to the households of parents than that of brothers; almost all the respondents were confident of reciprocity from parent's side, while a little more than one-third of the respondents expressed doubts about reciprocity from their brothers. Information collected indirectly also revealed that fraternal relations are based more on reciprocity than on considerations of blood relationship.

Migrant Respondents

A vast majority of migrant respondents (80.3%) reported having offered personal services to their parents on several occasions and also expressed their readiness to offer the same in future as well (Table 4.16). These included even those respondents who rarely visited their native place. The occasions on which they rendered personal services to their parents included their illness, the marriage of their (respondents) sisters and brothers, construction of house and wells, and 'shrad' ceremonies. The occasions on which they received services from their parents or from other dependent members mostly included the sickness of their wives or children and some other social ceremonies. Some of them also reported that their parents were readily willing to provide their personal services to them. Only a few respondents who had separated from their parents under uncordial conditions were neither willing to give nor receive personal services. The respondents who had not got any opportunity (17%) for rendering personal services expressed their readiness to do the same whenever such a need would arise. The respondents of these two categories together accounted for 97.3% of the total migrant respondents. It can be said conclusively that so far as the criterion of exchanging personal services (with parents) is concerned barring a few exceptions, almost all households of migrant respondents are closely related to the parents' households.

So far as the mutual exchange of personal services between the respondents and the households of their brothers is concerned we find that a majority of them (59.1%) are closely related as they reportedly help each other personally in case of need. If we add to it those (16.7%) who did not get an opportunity to receive or render personal services the percentage goes to 75.8. Some respondents (15.9%) expressed their willingness to exchange personal services but had not done so because of quarrels between their wives, separation under very uncordial circumstances, and time and cost involved in rendering such services.[5] Moreover, on the basis of this criterion, about three-fourths of the respondents turned out to be closely related to their brothers' households.

Conclusion

To conclude, if we look upon mutual exchange of services as a criterion of jointness, majority (88.5%) of the respondents' households may be considered as closely related to their affinal households. If one judges the jointness between the households on the basis of this criterion then most of the respondents' households are merely extension of a joint family. But because occasions for exchanging personal services have only rarely arisen, expression of mere willingness or even a rare exchange of service does not provide sufficient evidence for the close relationship between households.

Moreover, despite a fairly high degree of overall jointness, we find that it varies between native and migrant and also with regard to the households of parents and brothers. According to our findings the migrant respondents' household seemed to be more closely related to their affinal households in comparison to the households of native respondents. Besides, the households of both native and migrant respondents appeared to be relatively more closely related to the households of parents than that of brothers.

Joint Households

We have so far studied the extent of jointness between the respondents' nuclear households and the households of their parents and brothers living separately. This section is devoted to the study of functional relationship between different nuclear units constituting the joint households of the respondents. As already mentioned,[6] joint households cannot justifiably be straightaway treated as joint families. A household which is structurally or compositionally joint may not necessarily be functionally joint. We shall, therefore, study the joint households in the light of the criteria[7] of functional jointness.

Since members of a joint household live together, some of the criteria, such as reciprocal visits or rendering personal services, cannot be applied in this case. Since the respondent is himself the head in nearly half of the joint households, the question of seeking advice or approval too does not apply. Nevertheless, this aspect has been examined in the study of authority patterns, in the context of interpersonal relationships in Chapter V. These criteria would be relevant, had there been other households related to the respondents' joint household; the number of households related to the respondents' joint households in this case has been very small. Besides, the nature of relationships of the joint households having affinal relatives in separate households is such that one can straightaway determine whether the related households belong to the joint family or not.

The composition of joint households (Table 3.2) shows that almost all the members related by blood are living together in joint households with 5 exceptions in the case of migrant respondents and one in the case of native respondents. Out of 84 migrant respondents living in joint households, parents of only four and elder brother of only one lived at the village. The respondents expressed their eagerness to bring their parents to live with them in the city. Parents however wanted to stay at the village in an environment of their liking and had turned down the respondents' request to migrate to the city permanently. They however kept visiting the respondents' fraternally joint households at the latter's request. The respondents kept on sending money to their parents. Given this kind of relationship between the respondent and their parents both households can be said to be part and parcel of a joint family. In the solitary case of a brother living in the village, however, the relation is not cordial and the brothers' household is a nuclear household. Similar is the case with the solitary case of a brother of a native respondent living separately.

Thus it is only in the case of 2 respondents of joint households--one native and one migrant--that brothers of the respondents had functionally separated. Otherwise, all are joint structurally because the respondents parents and grand parents and brothers lived with him.

It is for this reason that there is little scope for studying the inter-household relationship on the basis of criteria other than fulfillment of mutual obligations. In this section, therefore, we shall confine our study of functional relationship between the members of joint households of both migrant and native respondents to only one criterion, i.e., fulfillment of financial obligations. In the context of joint households, fulfillment of financial obligation will mean mutual sharing of earnings by the members of a household or contribution to its 'common purse' without expecting any direct or proportionate benefit. In the traditional joint family earnings of all the members were pooled and generally spent by the eldest male member. The cardinal principle on which the institution of joint family was based is : 'From each according to his capacity to each according to his need'. Our aim here is to find out whether this principle conforms to the working of joint households of our respondents.

For judging jointness and establishing the kind of these households we adopted the following criteria:

(i) Households in which earning members hand over their salaries to the head who enjoys full authority to manage the household expenses have been considered as *joint families*.
(ii) In case members do not hand over their salaries to the head, and the household expenditure is shared according to the size of the nuclear units, the household will not be regarded functionally joint, even though apparently it may look so. For lack of a proper term, we shall regard these families as families in the process of nucleation.

The respondents have been divided into two categories on the basis of their position in the households:

(i) Respondents who are head of households, and
(ii) Respondents who are not heads of household.

Respondents as Heads of Household

Out of 112 joint households, 51 were headed by the respondents (Table 4.17 (A). Of these about 50% (25) enjoyed the position of a father living with their employed and married son(s); and their children. The remaining 26 respondents were the eldest brothers living with their married and earning younger brothers.

TABLE 4.17(A) : **Extent of Jointness in Joint Households by Nature of Household and Residential Background**

Sr. No.	Nature of Household	Households headed by Respondents								
		Migrants			Native			Total		
		Full*	Share@	Total	Full	Share	Total	Full	Share	Total
1	Lineal	16	4	20	3	2	5	19	6	25
		(80.0)	(20.0)	(100.0)	(60.0)	(40.0)	(100.0)	(76.0)	(24.0)	(100.0)
2.	Fraternal	10	14	24	1	1	2	11	15	26
		(41.7)	(58.3)	(100.0)	(50.0)	(50.0)	(100.0)	(42.2)	(57.8)	(100.0)
	Total	26	18	44	4	3	7	30	21	51
		(59.0)	(41.0)	(100.0)	(57.1)	(42.9)	(100.0)	(58.8)	(41.2)	(100.0)

* These are the households in which all the earning members hand over their salaries to the Head and he enjoys full authority to manage the household.

@ These are the households in which expenses are shared.

As in clear from the table (col. 8 and 9) the households of a majority (58.8%) of the respondents' joint households are not only joint households but joint families as well. All these respondents received full salaries from their son(s) in case of lineally joint households and brother(s) in case of fraternally joint households and enjoyed full freedom so far as the financial management of the household was concerned. The respondents would however pay pocket allowance to other earning members and there was full integration in the household. Though the majority of joint households are joint families, it is worth noting that quite a substantial percentage of households (41.2%) looking apparently joint families are not really so on the basis of this criterion. In the case of these respondents expenses are shared according to the size of the units. In these cases, nuclear units are together merely because they have no other alternative. These households have not been, therefore, considered as functionally joint families.

Though a majority of the households in the aggregate are joint families, there is a marked difference between lineal and fraternal jointness (col. 8): more than three-fourths (76.0%) of lineally joint households are joint families as well while the corresponding percentage in case of fraternally joint households is only 42.2. Some of the respondents of the fraternally joint households reported that with change in times the younger generation was becoming more conscious about their own nuclear units. They would not hesitate to separate from their brothers if they got the right kind of accommodation which was within their means. This indicates that fraternal jointness is on the decline and confirms our hypothesis that "the joint family pattern is expected to be prevalent less in fraternal than in lineal relations."

A comparative study on the basis of residential background reveals a significant difference in lineal jointness among the two categories: as many as 80% households of the migrant respondents are joint families, while corresponding figure for the native is only 60.0%.

Respondents Who Are Not the Heads

The respondents of this category are living either in lineally joint households or households which are lineally as well as fraternally joint or only fraternally joint. We grouped the first categories of respondents as one because both kinds of households are headed by parents or grand-parents. The remaining households are headed by the elder or eldest brother of the respondent.

Out of 112 joint households, those not headed by the respondents numbered 61; out of this 51 were headed by parents or grand-parents of the respondents and the remaining 10 by their elder or eldest brother. Since traditionally the earning members were expected to hand over their earnings to the head, the respondents were asked whether they followed such a practice and also whether the heads of their households were free to manage the household expenses according to their own wishes. Households of all those replying in the affirmative have been considered joint families functionally. The remaining cases in which expenses are shared according to the size of the nuclear units, in spite of joint residence, have not been considered as functionally joint families: these may be supposed to be in the process of nucleation.

The table (4.17B) indicates that the households of the majority of the respondents in this category were also functionally joint and accounted for about 79% (col. 8), while those which lacked functional jointness were 21.3%. Very insignificant variation in percentage figures existed between the lineally and fraternally joint households. A comparison on the basis of residential background is however quite revealing. As many as 90% lineally joint households of the migrant respondents were joint functionally as well, while the corresponding percentage for the native respondents was only 62. The over-all picture (Table 4.17C) is like this:

First, majority of the joint households (69.6%) are joint families as well. What is significant is that in spite of their apparent jointness, 30.4% joint households are not joint families; this indicates that a common residence cannot necessarily make a family joint.

Secondly, while more than three-fourths (75.6%) of lineally joint households are structurally as well as functionally joint families, the corresponding percentage for fraternally joint families is less than one-fourth (24.4%). This shows that lineal jointness exists in a larger measure than fraternal jointness.

TABLE 4.17(B) : **Households not headed by Respodents**

Sr. No.	Nature of Household	Migrants			Native			Total		
		Full*	Share@	Total	Full	Share	Total	Full	Share	Total
1		2	3	4	5	6	7	8	9	10
1.	Lineal	27 (90.0)	3 (10.0)	30 (100.0)	13 (61.9)	8 (38.1)	21 (100.0)	40 (78.4)	11 (21.6)	51 (100.0)
2.	Fraternal	8 (80.0)	2 (20.0)	10 (100.0)	- (-)	- (-)	- (-)	8 (80.0)	2 (20.0)	10 (100.0)
	Total	35 (87.5)	5 (12.5)	40 (100.0)	13 (61.9)	8 (38.1)	21 (100.0)	48 (78.7)	13 (21.3)	61 (100.0)

* These are the households in which all the earning members hand over their salaries to the Head and he enjoys full authority to manage the household.

@ These are the households in which expenses are shared.

TABLE 4.17(c) : **Extent of Jointness in Joint Households (Table A + B)**

S. No.	Nature of Household	Migrants			Native			Total		
		Full*	Share@	Total	Full	Share	Total	Full	Share	Total
	1	2	3	4	5	6	7	8	9	10
1	Lineal	43 (70.5)	7 (30.5)	50 (59.5)	16 (94.1)	10 (90.9)	26 (92.8)	59 (75.6)	17 (50.0)	76 (67.8)
2	Fraternal	18 (29.5)	16 (69.5)	34 (40.5)	1 (5.9)	1 (9.1)	2 (7.2)	19 (24.4)	17 (50.0)	36 (32.2)
	Total	61 (100.0)	23 (100.0)	84 (100.0)	17 (100.0)	11 (100.0)	28 (100.0)	78 (100.0)	34 (100.0)	112 (100.0)
		61 **(72.6)	23 (27.4)	84 (100.0)	17 (60.6)	11 (39.4)	28 (100.0)	78 (69.6)	34 (30.4)	112 (100.0)

* These are the households in which all the earning members hand over their salaries to the Head and he enjoys full authority to manage the household.

@ These are the households in which expenses are shared.

** These percentages are out of the respondents in each category - native and migrant.

Finally, overall jointness prevails in a larger measure among the migrant than among the native respondents: while about 73% of the migrant joint households are joint families functionally, households of only about 61% native respondents are functionally joint.

Summary

In the first part of this chapter we studied the causes of formation of 282 nuclear households (247 migrant and 35 native) and their functional relationship with other affinal households. The second part of the chapter deals with the functional relations between nuclear units constituting joint households.

Our study shows that the process of nucleation of households in the case of migrant started mostly with migration itself, which took place mainly on account of such economic reasons as inadequate sources of living in the village and/or the desire to earn additional income to support the members of the family at the village. Among the migrant 52.2% straightaway formed their nuclear households in the city. The remaining ones initially stayed with their brothers or parents forming a joint household, but later formed their nuclear households because of clashes and conflicts between the members of the household on such issues as sharing of household expenditure and household work. In case of native respondents, nearly 86% nuclear households were formed mainly because of clashes and conflicts between the members of the family and for lack of accommodation.

In all 46.8% cases of structural nucleation of households, both migrant and native, took place due to family quarrels and conflicts and in 53.2% cases nucleation took place due to paucity of land, the desire for earning additional income, and for want of adequate accommodation.

Applying four major aspects of functional relations--financial obligations, reciprocal visits, seeking advice and approval of elders, and rendering/exchange of personal services--to ascertain jointness we adopted various criteria with regard to each aspect chosen and the households were grouped under three categories: (i) Closely related, (ii) Marginally related, and (iii) Nuclear, and designated as families accordingly. The over-all findings are given in Table 4.18.

TABLE 4.18: Extent of Jointness Between Respondents and Their Parents and Brothers By Their Residential Background

S.No.	Extent of Jointness	Residential Background	Criterion (A) Feeling and fulfillment of financial obligation Type of relationship Parents	Brothers	(B) Reciprocal Visits Type of relationship Parents	Brothers	(C) Seeking advice and approval of elders Type of relationship Parents	Brothers	(D) Rendering/ Exchange of Personal Services Type of relationship Parents	Brothers
	1	2	3	4	5	6	7	8	9	10
1	Closely Related	Migrant	169	43	128	88	83	9	185	100
		Native	7	2	9	6	2	1	12	11
		Total	176	45	137	94	85	10	197	111
			(87.1)	(30.9)	(67.8)	(64.3)	(42.0)	(18.9)	(97.5)	(76.0)
2	Marginally Related	Migrant	13	36	46	20	99	12	-	21
		Native	2	2	2	3	7	3	1	2
		Total	15	38	48	23	106	15	1	23
			(7.4)	(26.0)	(23.7)	(15.7)	(54.4)	(28.3)	(0.5)	(15.8)
3	Nuclear	Migrant	6	53	14	24	6	24	3	11
		Native	5	10	3	5	5	4	1	1
		Total	11	63	17	29	11	28	4	12
			(5.5)	(43.1)	(8.5)	(20.0)	(5.6)	(52.8)	(2.0)	(8.2)
	Total	Migrant	188	132	188	132	188	45	188	132
		Native	14	14	14	14	14	8	14	14
		Total	202	146	202	146	202	53	202	146
			(100.0)	(100.0)	(100.0)	(100.0)	(100.0)	(100.0)	(100.0)	(100.0)

Sources: Col. 3 and 4, Table 4.7 Col. 5 and 6, Table 4.14
Col. 7 and 8, Table 4.15 Col. 9 and 10, Table 4.16

First, most of the nuclear households appear to be closely related to their affinal households. The percentage of households termed as closely related is much higher under all the aspects than the percentage of marginally related and nuclear households.

Secondly, there is a large difference between the percentage figures (total) related to parents and brothers. For instance while about 87% households are closely related to their parents, only about 31% are closely related to their brothers on the basis of feeling and fulfillment of financial obligations. This is largely true in regard to other aspects also. The functional relationship between the respondents and their parents is much stronger than between the fraternal households. This trend compares well with the trend indicated by the households of the other two categories. Besides, the percentage of respondents households termed as nuclear is much higher in respect of brothers than in respect of parents. All these figures put together indicate a higher degree of nucleation between fraternal households. This supports our hypothesis that "The joint family pattern is expected to be prevalent less in fraternal than in lineal relations".

Thirdly, in the case of both parents and brothers, the percentage of native households termed as closely related is much lower in respect of almost all the aspects of functional relations than the percentage of migrant households, with the exception of brothers in relation to seeking advice and approval. This pattern leads us to conclude that among native households the tendency towards nucleation is much greater in respect of both parents and brothers.

Fourthly, the households termed as marginally related are in the process of nucleation. Taking into view all the aspects of functional relations, on an average about one-third of respondents' households have either become nuclear or are in the process of nucleation vis-a-vis their parental households, and about half of them vis-a-vis their fraternal households.

Finally, not all the joint households which have the appearance of joint families turned out to be so when assessed on the basis of functional criterion. About 30% of them do not satisfy the criterion of functional jointness. Further, like nuclear households, functional jointness in fraternally joint households is much weaker when compared with lineally joint households. Also, migrant joint households have greater jointness than their native counterparts.

NOTES

1. This approach emphasises the study of the inter-household relationships between respondent's nuclear household and his filial and/or fraternal households, and between the constituent units of the respondents joint households.
2. Including the expenditure on litigation related to landed property.
3. The term elder here refers to father and, in his absence, elder brother.
4. On asking whether they expected the same from their brothers, 4 out of 11, had their own doubts about reciprocation as according to them the youngsters were 'modern' and did not care for anybody except their own nuclear unit. Respondents of elderly age-group, by and large, were not sure whether their younger brothers would care for them in time of need. One of the respondents observed that, not to speak of brothers the younger generation is good for nothing even for its parents. If they would be ready to serve the elders why would they think of separating which has become a way of life in the urban world.
5. In the case of respondents coming from far off places like eastern U.P. and Rajasthan.
6. See Chapter I
7. Applied to the study of functional relationship of nuclear households.

FIVE

Inter-Personal Relationships

In the preceding chapter we studied the functional relationship between the respondents' nuclear households and the households of their parents and brothers and also between the nuclear units that constitute joint households. In the present chapter, we intend to study the inter-personal relationships between the respondents and their kith and kin, who are of vital importance in the joint family system. For this we have focussed mainly on the authority pattern of the elders on the youngers; for the institutionalised authority pattern of elders has been one of the most important driving forces in the joint family. The authority pattern refers to the distribution of powers, responsibilities, and rights among the persons of different generations vis-a-vis others, which used to be of a hierarchical nature in the traditional Hindu joint family. Our attempt will, therefore, be to find out the present pattern of authority in the families of industrial workers, and then compare it with the traditional pattern to see whether there have been any changes in it or not. Its impact on the joint family system would also be assessed. This necessitates examining the authority pattern in the traditional joint family system.

The authority pattern in the Hindu joint family, as available in the existing literature on the subject, has been of a hierarchical nature. Age and sex were the most important considerations in the placement of a person in this hierarchy. Usually the eldest male member of a joint family used to be the head or the 'Karta' of the family; he enjoyed the highest position in the family structure. He was the centre of all power and other members were supposed to obey and pay regards to him; his decisions used to be final and binding on everybody. It was his sweet will to decide whether he would consult any other member of the family in discharging his functions. But he had authority to accept or reject the proposals or suggestions made by other member of the family: "The eldest male member (was) the centre of authority in the joint family" (Gore, 1968: 14). His powers, however, were not absolute and he could not use them arbitrarily; he had to exercise them in accordance with specific caste and family traditions and other conventional norms (Merton, 1957: 337-40). In the second generation the eldest son used to hold a superior position among the other male members of the family, but a position subordinate to the head and the elder woman. Among brothers, the eldest one was superior to his younger ones. Almost a similar pattern existed in regard to the female members of the family. So far as the relationship between males and females was concerned, the superiority pattern was determined on the basis of the generation one belonged to and the age of the husband in the case of women. But among males and females of the same generation, the male enjoyed a superior position in the family, provided, he was not a minor. Such a traditional authority pattern, however, cannot be expected to exist now because of the changing socio-economic conditions.

In earlier days a family used to function as a single unit both of production and consumption; there was hardly any spatial mobility. Even in the event of splitting up of the joint family, the nuclear units lived in each other's close vicinity. The elders could easily exercise their authority and supervise the activities of the youngsters. But, for such reasons as decrease in per capita land, inadequate means of livelihood, and a desire to have a better and independent living, on the one hand and opportunities provided by increasing industrialisation on the other there has been an increase in the mobility of people. This has led not only to splitting up of large families into nuclear units, but has also caused geographical separation between the units. This is expected to affect the authority pattern adversely: "The structure of authority, as the family moves from the joint to the nuclear form, weakens, and, as the small family units become separated from the large extended family group, comes to reside in each separate family unit "(Ross, 1961: 121).

Secondly, the geographical separation puts an end to the direct control of youngsters by the elders. The traditional kind of control ceases to exist.

Thirdly, the units moving away from the larger joint family get an opportunity to take decisions on a number of matters pertaining to day to day existence. In the process the head of the nuclear unit develops an independent outlook and a sense of authority, too, which may very often come in conflict with the authority of elders living separately and at a distance.

Fourthly, in the case of industrial workers, their physical mobility has been towards urban centres of growth. In an urban atmosphere they are bound to be influenced by the individualistic outlook of urban life. This is expected to make them less submissive to the authority of the elders of the family.

Finally, in earlier days the financial dependence of the younger ones on their elders for their livelihood, training, and acquiring of skill made them accept their authority. But independent living particularly of the migrants, makes them financially independent and, therefore, more assertive of their self assumed rights, which amounts to lessening of the authority of elders. It is probably because of all these developments that "inter-personal relationships more than ever before are becoming functionally specific" (Cheki, 1974: 226).

For the reasons mentioned above it may well be expected that the traditional authority has undergone a change or given way to a new pattern marked by reduced powers of elders over the youngsters. It is in the light of this hypothesis that we shall attempt a study of inter-personal relationships between the different sets of members related by birth or marriage in the family of industrial workers. Our main objective is to find out whether the existing pattern of authority in the family system of industrial workers has deviated from the norms of traditional authority pattern or not. Any deviation will be taken as an indicator of loss of authority of elders, which in turn will serve as an indicator of the weakening of the joint family system.

To study the authority pattern in the family system of industrial workers, we have chosen the following sets of relationships in a joint family system. The relationships between:

i. Father and son,
ii. Husband and wife,
iii. Mother, son, and daughter-in-law, and
iv. Brother and brother.

I

Father-son Relationship

The father-son relationship forms the basis of the joint family system and is the most important of affinal relationships. A son in a classic Hindu family was expected to be completely obedient to his parents, particularly his father. In conservative and rural societies the father had complete authority over his son, which he "exercised through rigorous discipline" (Kurian, 1961: 98). The father-son relationship was based on such an authoritative pattern that "it was his (father's) duty to command his sons and it was the duty of the sons to love and obey him" (Dhirendra Narain, 1970: 463). The normative pattern amongst Hindus was that a son could "not flout parents' will, especially not fathers" and the elders had an authority which could not be "lightly ignored by their children" (Mandelbaum, 1972: 39). A son was obedient to his father to the extent that he was not supposed even to seek clarification on matters on which the father had given orders.

This pattern of father-son relationship might have been followed not only because of traditional values or ideals laid down in religious scriptures which according to Suma Chitnis (1977: 18) "equated service of the parents with worship of gods", but also because of certain socio-economic conditions prevalent during the earlier times. First, occupational structure amongst Hindus was based on caste structure and heredity. A son was completely dependent on his father because he acquired his training through him and was dependent on the rich and ripe experience of his father, his professional skill, and efficiency. Secondly, the son was ordinarily bound to remain under the subordination of his father due to spatial and occupational immobility. During the earlier times, "the son grew into his father's profession, acquiring confidence and skill in the family business through an almost life-long association with his male relatives (D'Souza, 1972: 1), particularly with his father. A son had to depend on his father; naturally, he had to obey him. Such a relationship gave strength and sustenance to the institution of the joint family.

However, owing to numerous changes that have taken place in the socio-economic scene today, such as growing industrial expansion, development in the means of transport and communication, increasing population pressure on land in the rural areas, growing individualism, weakening of caste restrictions on the choice of occupation, and a number of other allied factors, there has been an increase in occupational and spatial mobility. These developments have reduced the control of the elders on the younger ones. "The increasing spread of education, occupational diversity and complexity and geographical and social mobility have been influencing the traditional kinship values and the behaviour patterns of the younger generation. The differences in ideas and ideologies and norms of family and kin behaviour between generations are widening" (Chekki, 1974: 224). These changes affect the father-son relationship because "when younger generation obtains new jobs and moves away from the village, it is able to assert its will in a much more effective fashion"(Goode, 1963: 248). Both father and son seem to be in a conflicting situation today, since "the father's main problem in a changing society is to gradually relinquish his position of dominant authority as his children grow older"(Ross, 1961: 101) and "the son (attempts) to emancipate himself from the dominance of parents" (Levy quoted by Ross, 1961: 99).

To study the father-son relationship the respondents were divided into two groups: (i) The respondent as a son, and (ii) the respondent as a father. The two main aspects of this relationship chosen are:

i. Authority of father over his sons, and
ii. Whether a father can rely on his sons for his maintenance when he retires or is not in a position to earn his own livelihood.

I. *Father's Authority*: When Respondent is a Son: Our main effort was to know the extent to which a son – the respondent – recognises the authority of his father. The general tests of such authority are: (i) love and respect for father, (ii) complete obedience to father, and (iii) financial dependence on father. Since all of our respondents were financially independent we limited our enquiry to the first two aspects of father's authority, i.e., love/respect and obedience. We found that the response in regard to these aspects was totally positive. Since we had no test for confirming the veracity of their response, we remodelled our questions, making them of an indirect nature, on the following aspects of relationship between father and son.

i. Whether the son (respondent) felt free to discuss matters with his father when he did not agree with his decisions.
ii. Whether the respondent complied with the restrictions imposed on him by his father.
iii. Whether the respondent referred his matters to his father when there was a difference of opinion between him (respondent) and any other member of the family, and did he accept his father as arbiter or not.

All the questions were not relevant to all the respondents. Out of 372[1] respondents, 63 reported not having had an occasion to refer any matter to fathers' arbitration; in 84 cases, fathers did not impose any restriction; they only gave advice. About two-thirds of the respondents felt free or did not hesitate in discussing matters concerning the problems of the family with their father. Although they said that it did not imply any lessening of respect for their father, it does indicate the desire of the respondents to share the power of decision-making with his father. This is in total contrast to the old days when sons would wait for the commands of their fathers.

Similarly we found that only about 78% comply with the restrictions imposed by their father, though in some matters, such as going to a movie or drinking liquor once in a while they did not just ignore their father. So far as accepting father as an arbiter in case of family quarrels and conflicts is concerned, only 80% reported accepting father's arbitration; nearly one-fifth of the respondents doubted their father's integrity as an arbiter. The overall picture is that obedience of a fairly high degree could be seen in about three-fourths of respondents. This trend can further be substantiated by looking into the attitude of the respondents on the basis of certain variables which may be taken as trend setters.

Residential Background and the Authority Pattern

We found that the migrant respondents were relatively more obedient to their fathers than their native counterparts. While only 67.6% migrant felt free to discuss matters with their fathers, the percentage among native was 83.3: the higher the freedom enjoyed in discussing matters with their father, the lower was the authority of the father in the traditional sense. The same is the case with regard to compliance with father's restrictions and accepting his verdict in case of differences or conflicts between the respondent and other members of the family. The difference in the percentages is indicative of the fact that the migrant, because of his rural back-ground is more obedient than native urban dwellers. The difference in the attitude is further verified by the difference in the percentages regarding the remaining two determinants of authority: 45% native respondents rarely complied with restrictions and 38.3% of them rarely accepted their father as arbiter; the corresponding percentages amongst migrant were 15 and 12.7 respectively. Also, the percentage of respondents never complying with father's restrictions or accepting his arbitership was much lower in case of migrant respondents than native ones.

Respondents reporting full obedience to their fathers restrictions or commands maintained that father should be given full respect and, therefore, they had always been obedient to them. Some of them, however, did so because of its social sanctity. Those reporting partial or rare compliance did so generally to keep their nuclear unit free from tensions; they felt that they could not ignore the wishes of wives and the interests of their children. This corroborates some of our earlier findings: the visits of the respondents to their native place had diminished because their children were not interested in continuing their links with their rural past.

A comparison between the percentage figures of the migrant and native respondents reveals that though the former were mostly attached to the traditional pattern, the latter were more individualistic and felt more concerned about their nuclear units. Migrant were of the opinion that the traditional order was bound to become weaker if younger generation kept migrating to the city and adopted the urban way of life which, according to them, was becoming a fashion. Though migration to the urban areas cannot be stated to be the only factor responsible for such a behaviour, it is apparent that the traditional pattern is gradually losing its hold on the urban population and its impact is clearly visible even amongst the migrant.

Respondents' Age and the Authority Pattern

A comparison between the age-groups of respondents (Table 5.1) shows that the older generation is still very much attached to the traditional pattern of authority, while the younger one is deviating from it. As many as 90% of the respondents of the youngest age-group (18-35) had always felt free to follow their ways; 10% had consulted their elders rarely. Amongst the middle-age group respondents (36-45) nearly half (48.2%) had always felt free to discuss different issues with their fathers, while 49% had done so rarely. The minimum percentage of respondents who had never enjoyed such freedom was 8.6%: they belonged to the oldest age group (46-60) followed by 2.8% among the middle age-group. There was none in this category from the respondents of the youngest age-group.

The age-group differential is however not equally divergent in the case of respondents who comply with the restrictions imposed by their fathers and accept them as arbiters. As many as 97.5% of the respondents of the oldest age group reported to have always complied with the restrictions imposed by fathers and accepted them as arbiter, and about 70% and 78% of the remaining two age-groups (18-35 and 36-45) respectively reported complying with restrictions imposed by fathers. Similarly, only about 73 and 82% of the respondents of 18-35 and 36-45 age-groups were ready to accept fathers as arbiters, and as many as 97.5% of the respondents of oldest age group (46-60) were prepared to do so.

TABLE 5.1: **Respondents' Attitude Towards Fathers Authority by Age**

S. No.	Determinants of fathers authority	Responses by Respondents' Age Group											
		Always			Rarely			Never			Total		
		(18-35)	(36-45)	(46-60)	(18-35)	(36-45)	(46-60)	(18-35)	(36-45)	(46-60)	(18-35)	(36-45)	(46-60)
1.	Feel/felt free to discuss matters	162 (90.0)	53 (48.2)	36 (43.9)	18 (10.0)	54 (49.0)	39 (47.5)	- (-)	3 (2.8)	7 (8.6)	180 (100)	110 (100)	82 (100)
2.	Comply/complied with restrictions imposed	124 (68.8)	86 (78.1)	80 (97.5)	50 (27.8)	22 (20.0)	2 (2.5)	6 (3.4)	2 (1.9)	- (-)	180 (100)	110 (100)	82 (100)
3.	Accept/accepted father as arbiter	131 (72.8)	90 (81.8)	80 (97.5)	43 (23.9)	18 (16.3)	2 (2.5)	6 (3.3)	2 (1.9)	- (-)	180 (100)	110 (100)	82 (100)

Note: The percentages are out of the total number of respondents in each age-group.

It is noteworthy that the younger generation seems to be relatively less obedient to parents than their older counterparts, though the difference between the obedience pattern of different age-groups is not very wide.

Our findings regarding the respondents of younger generation compare well with the findings of I.P. Desai and Kapadia (quoted by Goode, 1963: 249): "A considerable proportion of younger generation does not feel great restraint or awe with parents or guardians". Ross(1961: 135) also reports that "the elder generation no longer dominates the younger to the same degree or in the same way". Chekki's (1974: 224) observations also reveal that "respect and obedience to relatives older in age has been waning over the years". Such changes in the attitude of the younger generation towards the older generation are not expected to leave the traditional authority pattern unaffected. It is noteworthy that even amongst the migrant the deviants belong to the youngest age-group who have been in the city since their childhood. Some of the respondents of this age-group were critical of the elder generation and observed that trouble arose only when the elderly people failed to note the change in times.

Nature of Household and the Authority Pattern

A comparison of the percentage figures of the household and their attitude towards the authority of a father clearly brings out nuclear-joint differential: respondents living in joint households, though not completely tradition-oriented, are more attached to the traditional pattern than their counterparts in nuclear households. More than three-fourths (76.2%) respondents of the nuclear households had always felt free to discuss matters with their fathers, while less than half (45.8%) of the respondents belonging to the joint households always enjoyed such freedom. The percentage of those enjoying such freedom rarely was 52.3 amongst the respondents of the joint households and only 20.7 in the respondents of nuclear households. This shows that the nuclear households have become more individualistic and, therefore, feel free to discuss issues with their fathers, which is against the traditional norm.

The difference can also be seen in respondents' attitudes towards compliance with restrictions imposed by father and accepting him as arbiter. About 86% joint household respondents reported always complying with the restrictions imposed and 93.4% accepted their father as arbiter; the corresponding percentages of respondents of nuclear households are 74.7 and 75.8. Further, while only 12% and 4.5% of joint household respondents did so rarely, the corresponding percentages of the respondents of nuclear household were 23 and 22 respectively.

Our findings were similar to those of Ross's (1961: 132) findings that "when the large extended family breaks down, the authority of the patriarch gradually diminishes, and each individual family unit eventually becomes an independent self governing unit."

Our study of father-son relationship reveals that the traditional authority of father over the son does exist, but not in its traditional form: it has become considerably diluted. We also found that father's authority in the case of native respondents is much weaker than in the case of migrant respondents. In both the categories the younger generation has much less regard for father's authority than older one. Also, the respondents living in nuclear households have relatively less regard for father's authority than those living in joint households. It seems with spatial and occupational mobility, structural nucleation of households and financial independence, a considerable change has taken place in the traditional norms of father's authority in a family.

Father's Authority: When respondent in Father

In this sub-section we have studied the authority pattern on the basis of the same determinants when our respondent is the father of major and earning sons. This will help us in making a comparative study of two stages involving three generations. The study would have been more illuminating had the number of respondents having earning sons been approximately equal to the number of respondents studied in relation to father, but the two figures were not comparable. While the number of respondents (being sons) studied in relation to father was 372, only 35 respondents (being father) could be studied in relation to sons.

Our enquiry is based on the same set of questions used in case of respondents being sons. Here the respondents (fathers) were asked whether their sons felt free to discuss family matters with them, complied with the restrictions imposed by them, and also whether their arbitratorship was acceptable to them when there were conflicts in the family.

Sons of 83% respondents always felt free to discuss family matters with them, while only 67% respondents always enjoyed such freedom; 78 and 81% of respondents reportedly always complied with the restrictions imposed by their father and accepted him as arbiter, the corresponding percentages of respondents' sons doing so was only 48.5 and 57.2. Besides, respondents' sons who comply with the restrictions rarely or never and are rarely or never prepared to accept father's arbitration are much larger in proportion than in the case of the respondents themselves in this context.

To conclude, our findings reveal that there is a gradual increase in the assertiveness of the young ones which would result in the loss of father's traditional authority over his son. If it continues the traditional pattern of father's authority over his son is bound to diminish in future.

Future Trend

Yet another attempt was made to find out if there would be a further loss in father's authority in future. The behaviour of minor children can legitimately be taken as a fairly good indicator of their future adult behaviour. Following this hypothesis we asked the respondents whether or not they observed any differnces in the general bahaviour of minor children of today when compared with their own behaviour when they were children. Only 72 out of 394 respondents denied having observed any significant difference. The remaining 322 respondents were asked to mention the differences observed. Their responses are presented in table 5.2.

The most significant difference reported by the respondents (67.7%) was that children of today demanded more freedom than the respondents had ever asked for. The respondents of elderly age-group were very critical of such a tendency and feared that the future generation would hardly have any respect for age. The second

TABLE 5.2: **Differences Observed in the General Behaviour of Children** (Responses)

S.No.	Differences observed	Number of responses	Percentage to Total (322)*
1.	Demand more freedom	218	67.7
2.	Less tolerant	152	45.8
3.	Less obedient	122	37.8

* Out of 394 respondents only 322 reported observing differences in the general behaviour of children. Since some of the respondents reported more than one difference the number of responses exceeds the number of respondents.

major change reported was that the children of today had become less tolerant which has resulted in diminished respect for age. This was the opinion of about 46% respondents. Another noticeable change reported was decreasing obedience of children to their elders. There were no significant variations on the basis of different variables. A general opinion of the respondents, particularly of older age, was that if the same trend continued the elders would lose control over the coming generation completely. They were critical of the manner in which young children were being brought up by their parents.

TABLE 5.3 : **Causes for Differences in Behaviour of children**

S. No.	Causes for differences	Number of responses	Percentage to Total (322)
1.	Lack of moral education	182	56.5
2.	Cinema	166	51.5
3.	Modern social environment	130	40.3
4.	Lack of parental supervision	34	10.5

Note: Since some respondents reported more than one causes, number of responses exceeds the number of respondents.

The most important cause (Table 5.3) reportedly responsible for the difference in the behaviour of children in the past and present was lack of moral education (56.6%). The introduction of formal education which did not attach any importance to moral and religious education was said to be responsible for causing drastic changes in the temperament and manners of children. They stated that in their days of youth religious teaching was imparted in the families through mythological tales[2], and 'Kathas' and 'Kirtans' at regular intervals, which moulded children's attitude towards obedience to elders, whereas with the growth of formal education this teaching had almost disappeared. Nearly half of the respondents (51.5%) felt that movie going was responsible for spoiling children. Those blaming modern social environment (40.3) for such differences reported that parents could not afford to be harsh to their children as they feared the consequences of such a treatment.[3] A few of the respondents (10.5%) attributed this difference to lack of parental supervision.

If childhood behaviour is any indication of the future adult behaviour the children of today should not be expected to be as obedient as the earlier ones were. This will certainly undermine father's authority.

Old Age Security

The institution of the joint family in its traditional form worked as an agency of social security for the aged and the infirm: "The aged and the infirm were assured of shelter, care and protection" (D' Souza, 1972: 1). It was considered to be the pious duty of a son to look after his aged parents. Since both -- parents and children -- would ordinarily live together the son just could not ignore his parents. The entire family worked as "an ordered network of relationships between individuals bound by duty, obligation and affection." But "The dynamics of human society are such that the definition of rights and responsibilities in each of the several areas of life in which individuals participate...are constantly changing" (Suma Chitnis, 1977: 18). In the changing circumstances the individual is becoming self-centred and indifferent towards the responsibilities which have devolved on him through tradition. As such, people are said to have become indifferent towards their parents, especially when they are not in a position to earn their living. Keeping this in mind we tried to find out the opinion of respondents about their responsibilities towards parents, especially father, when he is not in a position to earn.

We avoided putting direct questions to the respondents because there was the danger of getting biased answers. We asked them whether a father, after he was not in a position to earn, should depend on his son, be on his own, or be the responsibility of the state. Only about 49% reported that looking after ones father was the duty of a son; 36% opined that fathers, should make their own arrangements for old age; and the remaining 15% wanted the state to look after the aged.

This shows that nearly half of the respondents (48.7%) are still attached to tradition. Most of them belonged to joint households.They were of the opinion that a father who had spent all his savings on the well being of his children deserved to be cared for. State should take care of only those old people who did not have any sons to look after them. Some of the respondents in this category observed that people who did not look after their parents should be condemned by the community. More than one-third (36.0%) of the respondents felt that people should save for their old age; they mostly belonged to the older age-group. A few of them remarked on the basis of their own and their colleague's experience that not to speak of non-earning old people, even those who are in a position to earn are not looked after by their sons after they were married. Some of them who were about to retire regretted having spent their hard earned money on the marriage of their sons who had separated after a few years after their marriage. This is clearly a deviation from the traditional norm. Only 15% felt old people should be taken care of by the state. They included respondents of all age-groups, both native and migrant and the ones living in nuclear and joint households.

The most significant fact to be noted in this regard is that only about half of the respondents feel it to be the responsibility of the son(s) to look after their fathers in their old age, whereas in earlier times it was the first and foremost duty of a son. Besides, while earlier people did everything possible to beget a son as an old-age security, now more than one-third respondents have no hope of relying on their sons in their old age. These responses are a significant deviation from the traditional norm.

II

Husband-Wife Relationship

Another relationship which is important for the continuation of nuclear as well as joint family is that of husband and wife. In the traditional joint family husband-wife relationship was strong and comparatively stable because of two reasons: (i) Lower status of wives vis-a-vis their husbands, and (ii) subordination of conjugal bond to consanguineal bond.

According to Hindu law-giver Manu and other Smriti writers, a wife is "to obey her lord as long as he lives, and remain faithful to his memory after his death" (Prabhu, 1963: 231). Abbe Dubois (quoted in Dhirendra Narain, 1970: 457) provides a detailed account of the rules of conduct of married women from Padmapuran:" a wife should always look upon him [her husband] as her God, should lavish on him all her attention and care, paying no heed whatsoever to his character and giving him no cause whatsoever for his displeasure". Describing the traditional pattern of husband-wife relations, Mandelbaum (1972: 38) points out that " a husband is expected to be his wife's superior and to receive symbolic and actual deference from her".

Such a man-woman relationship existed not merely because it had a religious sanction but also because it was an established custom. The custom of child marriage, a big gap in the age of husband and wife, comparative illiteracy and ignorance of wives and their economic dependence on their husbands contributed largely to the continuity of such a relationship between them.

The second characteristic of this husband-wife relationship, which was also helpful in sustaining the joint family, was the subordination of conjugal bond to the consanguineal bond. This was because of child marriage and segregation of sexes. Every effort was made in the traditional joint family to keep the two at a distance and permitting them to meet only during nights. Hitchcock notes: "A husband is not supposed to show any open concern for his wife's welfare; this is the responsibility of his parents. If the wife is sick, the mother-in-law and father-in-law see that she goes to a doctor, if they do not, neither she nor her husband should complain" (Dhirendra Narain, 1970: 458). It was not considered desirable for "a young man to show interest in or concern for his wife in front of others" (Vatuk, 1972: 113-114). Under such circumstances development of close emotional relationships between husband and wife was very rare, if not totally impossible.

But in modern times, things have changed considerably. Many young people are migrating to cities affecting the structure of joint family by breaking it into nuclear units; these are bound to change the pattern of husband-wife relations. "The husband-wife relation changes radically when the family system alters from joint to nuclear" (Ross, 1961 : 161). In such families, as Yogendra Singh (1973: 183) points out "the wife becomes the most important agent around whom the whole activity revolves". This leads to a very close emotional relationships between husband and wife; which, in turn disrupts man's filial and fraternal duties, and ultimately affects the joint family system not only from the structural but also from the functional point of view. Yogendra Singh (1973: 183-84) is also of the opinion that when there is "transition from joint to nuclear families... affective bonds between husband and wife become more particularised and become intense, and bonds uniting collateral relatives tend to be weakened, *thus altering the very structure of joint family* sentiments" (emphasis mine). Besides, the rising status of women[4] due to their higher age at marriage, increase in education, influence of urban environment and the increasing possibility of their economic independence are expected to make the women more assertive and less docile than before.

In view of the foregoing discussion we may now state our hypothesis: The changing relations between husband and wife would bring them closer to each other and this is expected to strengthen the conjugal relations and consequently weaken their subordination to consanguineal relations. This would ultimately be a threat to the traditional joint family system. It is with this hypothesis that we intend to study the existing pattern of husband-wife relations in our respondents. The main areas of our enquiry would be: (i) The subordination and obedience of wife to her husband, (ii) Husband's right to scold his disobedient wife, (iii) Right of wife to interfere in her husband's activities, and (iv) Occurence of conflicts between the two and their causes and consequences.

So far as the wife's obedience to her husband is concerned it conformed to the traditional pattern. 97.5% of wives were obedient to their husbands. The remaining 2.5% were only partly obedient to them. A good deal of deviation from the traditional norm could be observed in the remaining three aspects. The majority of the respondents (62.1%) observed that wives should neither be prepared to accept nor be assigned a position subordinate to their husbands. Likewise, regarding the husband's right to scold his wife, a little more than two-third of them were of the opinion that the husbands do possess the right to scold their wives when they do something which was not liked by them. Even then wives did not quietly tolerate the scolding as they did during the earlier days; they would argue with their husbands. Very often it would breed tension between them. 65% respondents said that wives had every right to interfere in their husband's activities.

To sum up the traditional form of husband-wife relationship, in which a wife was subordinate to her husband, is gradually giving way to a more egalitarian relationship. To see these in a perspective, we shall now analyse the opinions of the respondents on the basis of their age, nature of household, and residential background.

Age of the Respondent and Husband-Wife Relations

The most significant variations in the responses were found in the age-groups of the respondents (Table 5.4). Only about one-fifth (19.1%) of the respondents in the youngest age group were of the opinion that wife is subordinate to her husband, while the corresponding percentages of the respondents of middle and older age-group were 44.3 and 68.4 respectively. The same trend is repeated in regard to the husband's right to scold his wife in case she did anything against the wishes of her husband. Only 13.8% of the respondents of younger generation favoured the proposition, while it increased to 34.6% in the case of the middle age group, and to 67.3% in case of the respondents of older age group.

TABLE 5.4 : **Aspects of Husband-wife Relationship by Respondents' Age, Nature of the Household and Residential Background**

S. No.	Aspects of Relationship	Responses by Age Group						Responses by Nature of Household				Responses by Residential Background			
		(18-35)		(36-45)		(46-60)		Nuclear		Joint		Native		Migrant	
		Yes	No	Yes	No	Yes	No	Yes	No	Yes	No	Yes	No	Yes	No
I	Wife is subordinate to husband	36 (19.1)	153 (80.9)	50 (44.3)	63 (55.7)	63 (68.4)	29 (31.6)	71 (25.2)	211 (74.8)	78 (69.6)	34 (30.4)	15 (23.9)	48 (76.1)	134 (40.5)	197 (59.5)
II	Wife's obedience to husband	181 (95.2)	8 (4.8)	111 (98.1)	2 (1.9)	92 (100.0)	- (-)	274 (97.1)	8 (2.9)	110 (97.3)	2 (2.7)	59 (93.6)	4 (6.4)	325 (98.1)	6 (1.9)
III	Husband's right to scold wife	26 (13.8)	163 ((86.2)	39 (34.6)	74 (65.4)	62 (67.3)	30 (32.7)	65 (23.1)	217 (76.9)	62 (55.3)	50 (44.7)	11 (17.5)	52 (82.5)	116 (35.1)	215 (64.9)
IV	Wife has right to interfere in husbands activities	157 (83.0)	32 (17.0)	72 (63.7)	41 (36.3)	29 (31.6)	63 (68.4)	220 (78.0)	62 (22.0)	38 (34.0)	74 (66.0)	50 (79.3)	13 (20.7)	208 (62.5)	123 (37.5)

Note: Percentages are out of the number of respondents in each category.

On wife's right to interfere in the activities of her husband as many as 83% of the respondents of the youngest age group approve of her interference. Only 63.7% of the respondents of middle age group favoured this interference; in the older age-group only one-third approved the idea.

The overall picture that emerges from age as a variable clearly indicates that the younger generation is prepared to give woman a status higher than what it was in the traditional order: they do not consider the wife subordinate but equal. This poses a threat to the joint family.

Nature of Household and Husband-wife relations

The nature of household to which one belongs also makes a difference in one's attitude towards husband-wife relations. Those belonging to nuclear households are expected to be less attached to the traditional norms of husband-wife relationship than those belonging to joint households. Only one-fourth of the respondents living in nuclear households favoured the traditional pattern of assigning a lower status to the wife vis-a-vis her husband, while the percentage of such respondents from among joint households was 69.6. Similarly, only 22.1% of the workers living in nuclear households thought that the husband had a right to scold his wife, while more than half (55.3%) of joint householders thought so. So far as wife's right to interfere in the activities of husband was concerned the trend appeared to be the same i.e., most of the respondents (78%) of nuclear households thought that wife had a right to interfere while amongst those living in joint households only 34.0% favoured it. This implies that workers living in joint households are more tradition-bound than those living in nuclear households.

Residential Background and Husband-Wife Relations

The rural-urban differential is also quite revealing. Native respondents were against the traditional pattern as compared to their migrant counterparts. Only about one-fourth of native respondents opined that wife had a subordinate position vis-a-vis her husband while the corresponding percentage amongst migrant was

40.5. Similarly, only 17% native respondents favoured the idea of husbands giving a scolding to wives, while the percentage of migrant having this view was nearly double (35.1%). Almost about 80% native respondents thought that wife had a right to interfere in the activities of her husband while the corresponding percentage amongst migrant was only 62.5.

To sum up, the foregoing discussion indicates change in the traditional pattern of husband-wife relations. The change is more evident amongst the respondents of younger generation, native, and those living in nuclear households as compared with their counterparts. Though the majority of the respondents of the latter categories expressed their faith in the traditional pattern, even among those a substantial number of respondents was found to be critical of the traditional pattern.

The tendency towards egalitarian relations between husband and wife can further be verified on the basis of the nature of the causes of conflicts between them. Only 111 out of 394 respondents reported disagreements and disputes between them and their wives. The causes of conflicts are of two categories: (i) those pertaining purely to personal affairs between husband and wife and their children, and (ii) those arising out of their relationship with husband's lineal or fraternal relatives. In the case of our respondents, conflicts of the first category were rare : only 19 out of 111 couples had quarreled on account of purely personal reasons: these include non-fulfillment of certain demands of wife, difference over the treatment of children, selection of parties for children's marriage, taking liquor by the respondent, and on the question of giving higher education to daughter or getting her married. 83% of the respondents quarreled with their wives because of their involvement with respondents lineal and/or fraternal relatives. About 37% quarreled with their wives on the issue of sending money to other relatives and 36% on account of wife's insistence on separating from the lineal or fraternal relatives. The other reason was husband's insistence on keeping some member of the kinship group in his nuclear household. Quarrels on these accounts do indicate that wives are becoming more assertive and tend to overrule their husbands.

This changed position of wife vis-a-vis her husband is further confirmed by looking into the figures pertaining to the consequences of disagreements or disputes. In such disputes 55.8% respondents prevailed upon their wives and the wives had to reconcile. About 40% reported that they had to reconcile to their wives. In the remaining 5.5% cases the disagreements persisted. Where the husbands reconciled, most of them felt that their wives had adopted the right course; only a few reconciled to avoid further clashes. This indicates that with changing times wives will have a relationship of equality with their husbands which would threaten the continuation of the joint family.

III

Mother-Son and Mother-in-Law and Daughter-in-Law Relationships

Another important set of relationship having a significant bearing on the existence of the joint family is the triangular one between a man, his wife and his mother. The two sets of relationships formed by their involvement are: (i) mother-in-law and daughter-in-law, and (ii) mother and son. The first of the two is said to be the most important for the continued existence of a joint family since it determines the nature of the organisation and working of a joint family. By virtue of her age and relatively higher position in the family the mother-in-law held the power of governance over her daughter-in-law. The loyalty of the son towards his mother, which was based not only on traditional belief but was "upheld in the actuality of the family life" (Mandelbaum; 1972: 62), further strengthened her position. Besides, a number of other institutional factors such as child marriage, process of mate-selection, subordination of conjugal relations to consanguineal relations, status of bride in the new households and segregation of sexes kept the daughter-in-law closer to and under the subordination of her mother-in-law than her husband.[5]

Under the traditional authority pattern, the mother-in-law decided the course of life for her daughter-in-law; she would take care of her interest in regard to her basic requirements, control and regulate her activities and behaviour, and protect her against any offence from other members of the family. She would also decide the frequency of her visits to her parent's house. The daughter-in-law had to offer full obedience to her mother-in-law (including doing jobs for her, such as washing her clothes, massaging her body in the evening). Not merely that. She virtually shaped the pattern of her existence.

This pattern worked smoothly for a long time because it had social sanction and was accepted without any questioning by both the parties. However, deviations from the accepted norm, whether in the form of excessive use of power by mother-in-law or the insolence and disobedience of daughter-in-law led to clashes and conflicts: "The classic and current Indian literature pictures the relationship as one in which the daughter-in-law often feared and hated her mother-in-law and latter in turn was extremely jealous of her as a rival for her son's affection" (Ross, 1961: 170) In some cases it became so intolerable that daughter-in-law was driven to suicide (Srinivas, 1942 : 197). The relationship has also been looked upon as the one between two "natural enemies" (Karve, 1965: 130)

This unpleasant aspect of the relationship between the two seems to have been overemphasised, "for if the conflict had been as constant and severe as suggested, the traditional joint family could not have borne the strain (Ross, 1961 :170). Nevertheless, the fact remains that it often led to strain, which sometimes led to bifurcation in the family. This, however, was an exception. The rule was that in spite of conflicts and quarrels and hostility between the two, the authority of the mother-in-law over her daughter-in-law prevailed and she was supported by her son's loyalty: "In the traditional family a man was expected to be closer to his mother than to his wife" (Kapadia, 1966: 267). These sustained the joint family for a long time.

One can however presume that the traditional authority of mother-in-law cannot remain unaffected because of changed social climate. First, with the migration of younger generation with its nuclear units from rural to the urban areas, the possibility of a stronger emotional bond between husband and wife cannot be ruled out. This will weaken filial bonds and strengthen conjugal bonds, which weakens mother's authority over her daughter-in-law.

Secondly, due to increase in age-at-marriage a bride now enters her new household relatively at an advanced age with better education than her mother-in-law. With this background she can hardly be expected to be as docile and submissive as she used to be earlier. The daughter-in-law may become status conscious, and "With increasing consciousness about her role and status, a contemporary daughter-in-law will not take [her subjugation] passively" (Ramanujam, 1972 :29). Moreover, such a daughter-in-law "dares to disagree with her mother-in-law and persuades her husband to separate from the parental household" (Vatuk, 1972 : 69). Also, "the new emphasis on love between husband and wife means that the mother will no longer have first place in the son's affections" (Ross, 1961 : 152). This leads to strain in the substructure of authority in the relationship of "... mother, son and daughter-in-law triangle" (Ross, 1961 : 135). In such situations" [man's] position becomes really difficult when he is subjected to pressure simultaneously from two directions when the mother complains about his wife and the wife complains about the mother"(Dube, 1965 : 143). Any shift in bond loyalty, we assume, would affect mother's position adversely and in turn affect the mother-in-law and daughter-in-law relationship too.

For studying the mother-in-law and daughter-in-law relationship, the best procedure would have been to interview the women from the industrial workers' households. Since that could not be possible, we collected information from our respondents by putting questions to them to find out: (i) whether man today is closer to his wife or to his mother, and (ii) what he felt about mother-in-law daughter-in-law relations on the basis of his personal experiences. Other enquiries made in this regard were: (i) whether their wives worked according to the instructions of their mothers, (ii) in case it was not so, whether it resulted in conflicts, and (iii) the role that a son could play in such situations, as also the role they had themselves played when confronted with such situations.

The final assessment of mother-in-law and daughter-in-law and mother and son relation was made on the basis of enquiries in their entirety. An effort was also made to find out the deviations, if any, from the traditional values and to indicate future trends on that basis and also on the basis of other variables.

Respondents' observations about Peoples Closeness to Mother/Wife

First of all, the respondents were asked about their observations regarding people's closeness to their mothers and wives. About 54% of the respondents reported that people still adhere to the 'traditional value' of being closer to their mothers. One-third of the respondents (33.2%), however, stated that because of change in times, there had been a deviation from the traditional pattern and that people were generally observed to be closer to their wives than to their mothers. The remaining 13% said that people were equally close to both mothers and wives.

Another noteworthy feature about the respondents' general observation was that most of the respondents who reported increasing trend of closeness towards wives belonged to the elderly age-group. Their observations, as they reported, were based on behaviour patterns of their acquaintances, people in their locality and their relatives. They blamed urban atmosphere and the popularity of cinema for such a changing trend. Both these factors, according to them, had led to enormous increase in sexual stimulation, which had forged closeness between husband and wife and made sons indifferent towards their mothers. Nearly half of the respondents (46.2%) felt that people were deviating from the traditional norm because they were either closer to their wives or equally close to wives and mothers.

Respondents' Closeness to Mother/Wife

Here we intend to analyse the respondents' closeness to their mothers vis-a-vis their wives. Only respondents married during the life-time of their mothers are included in the analysis. Majority of the respondents (68.1%) reported that they were closer to their mothers than to their wives. This is at variance with the pattern amongst the main sample of Agarwals in whom only 56% respondents were found to be closer to mothers (Gore, 1968 : 176). Most of the respondents who reported being closer to their mothers belonged to the elderly age-group and reported that they had been brought up in an atmosphere in which mothers were revered and respected. Respondents closer to their wives and those equally close to their mothers and wives accounted for 13.7 and 18.2% respectively. Most of the respondents of the former category blamed their mothers for this because they thought that they were very harsh to their daughters-in-law. One of the respondents, for instance reported that his wife was barren and for that reason was condemned by his mother. Out of resentment, he separated from his parents for good. Those reporting equal closeness to both mothers and wives justified their behaviour on human grounds; they felt that both deserved importance. They did not favour the authoritarian attitude of the mother-in-law and felt that daughter-in-law had genuine grievances against them. This can convincingly be taken as an indication of a gradual deviation from the traditional pattern. Deviations studied in the light of residential background and the nature of the respondents household (Table 5.5) do indicate the likely future trends.

TABLE 5.5: **Respondents' Closeness to Mother/Wife; by Residential Background and Nature of Household**

S. No.	Relation-ship	Residential Background			Nature of Household		
		Native	Migrant	Total	Nuclear	Joint	Total
1.	Closer to Mother	31 (67.3)	200 (68.2)	231	153 (62.1)	78 (83.8)	231
2.	Closer to Wife	8 (17.3)	38 (12.9)	46	39 (16.0)	7 (7.6)	46
3.	Equally close to both	7 (15.4)	55 (18.9)	62	54 (21.9)	8 (8.6)	62
	Total	46 (100.0)	293 (100.0)	339	246 (100.0)	93 (100.0)	339

Residential Background and Closeness to Mother/Wife

Contrary to the general belief that an urban dweller is more close to his wife than to his mother, our study does not show any significant native-migrant differential amongst industrial workers. Two-thirds of the respondents in both the categories reported to be closer to their mothers. Native respondents closer to their wives and those equally close to mothers and wives accounted for 17.3 and 15.4% respectively, while the corresponding percentages for the migrant are about 13 and 19. Nevertheless, the general impression gathered during the course of interview revealed that the native were less keen on adhering to the traditional values than their migrant counterparts, which is supported by variation in percentages of the latter two types of responses.

Nature of Household and Closeness to Mother/Wife

Nature of household is also expected to have its impact on the nature of relation between man and his wife and man and his mother. Living continuously with one's mother in a joint household may bring mother and son closer to each other, giving subordinate position to the daughter-in-law. At the same time the possibility of uncordial relations between the two can also not be ruled out: staying together may afford more chances of conflict resulting in closeness between man and his wife. Likewise, living with wife in a separate household can also have its impact on mother-son relation as one may not maintain the same closeness towards mother as is traditionally expected or by eliminating chances of conflict the two may come closer emotionally. It has generally been observed that living in a nuclear household--separate from mother--increases conjugal intimacy, leading to the supremacy of conjugal relations to consanguineal ones and ultimately affecting mother-son relations: "The husband-wife relation changes radically when the family system alters from joint to nuclear...[and] the growing strength of the husband-wife relationship in smaller family units definitely tends to weaken the affectionate tie between mother and son " (Ross, 1961 : 161-72). It is for these reasons that responses have also been tabulated on the basis of respondents nature of household.

Table (5.5) brings out the nuclear-joint differential: about 84% of the respondents living in joint households reported to be closer to their mothers, while the corresponding percentage amongst those in nuclear households is 62. The difference between percentage figures is indicative of the fact that in the joint households mother-son relationship continues to be tradition-oriented; respondents reported that they could not think of separating from their mothers. A few of them were residing jointly in spite of the repeated insistence of their wives for living separately. Nuclear-joint differential is further supported by the percentage of respondents closer to their wives:

only 7.6% respondents in joint households reported to be closer to their wives while more than its double (16%) reported so amongst respondents in nuclear households.

The intensity of mother-son bond was further examined by asking the respondents whether or not one's increasing responsibilities of nuclear units affected adversely the closeness between mother and son. According to majority of the respondents mother-son bond remained unaffected, quite a few of them did observe that increasing responsibilities, coupled with unaccommodating nature of mothers and wives decidedly affected the mother-son bond. Some of the respondents who had earlier reported to be closer to their wives categorically stated that when the tradition-oriented mother failed to adjust with her daughter-in-law they ultimately got detached from their mother. Respondents of elder age group were very critical of the younger generation and stated that younger people forgot parents soon after their marriage.

To conclude, though the majority of the respondents were closer to their mothers, those equally close to both mothers and wives and even those closer to wives were not nonexistent. Respondents reporting to be closer to wives and living in nuclear households sufficiently indicate that mother-in-law is not in a position to enjoy traditional authority over her daughter-in-law as was the case earlier. Taking into account the factors already at work--the structural nucleation of households and the number of people closer to wives or even closer to both mother and wife, the traditional authority pattern among females is leaning towards a radical shift.

Obedience of Daughter-in-law

The existence of quite a substantial number of deviants from the traditional pattern of mother-son relations, and the respondents' observations about mother-son v/s husband-wife relations indicated a shift in bond loyalty between mother and son which presumably affect the authoritative position of mother-in-law. Inferentially this would reduce the obedience of the former to the latter. Therefore, to have a proper assessment of the obedience of daughter-in-law to mother-in-law the respondents having mothers and wives alive were asked whether their wives were obedient to their (respondents') mothers. These inquiries revealed the continuation of the traditional practice of the obedience of daughter-in-law to her mother-in-law to a large extent: about two-thirds (68.1%) of the respondents reported that their wives were always obedient to their mothers. Wives of more than one-fifth (22.2%) of the respondents obeyed their mothers occasionally; only in the case of 8.0% was obedience a rare phenomenon. A negligible percentage of respondents' (1.7%) wives never cared to be obedient to their (respondents') mothers.

What is noteworthy is that daughters-in-law who lived separately were proportionately more obedient than those who lived with their mothers-in-law. Nearly three-fourths (71.1%) of the daughters-in-law of the former category were reported to be obedient to their mothers-in-law 'always', while the corresponding percentage from the latter category was only 54.3. This indicates that if daughters-in-law are made to live with their mothers-in-law their obedience will decrease and the obedience of daughter-in-law living separately is only casual and a ritualistic behaviour not genuine. If the authority pattern followed in these households is any indication of the existing situation, it seems that compared with the traditional situation mothers-in-law are losing their hold on daughters-in-law.

Role of Man between Mother and Wife

In case of a conflict between mother-in-law and daughter-in-law tradition demanded man to side with his mother. To find out the present trend, the respondents were asked whether a man should favour his mother or wife or remain indifferent. More than three-fourths (77.9%) of the respondents said that a man should always favour his mother, whatever be the cause of conflict and whosoever be at fault. Nearly one-fifth (18.2%) of the respondents pleaded for remaining indifferent. This they thought would lessen the possibilities of further conflict. Some of them were not in favour of adopting the traditional attitude of favouring the mother blindly. They pleaded for daughter-in-law's right to lead a respectable life, and did not favour the exploitative attitude adopted by some mothers-in-law. A very small percentage (3.9%), however, were in favour of siding with their wives. These respondents generally belonged to the younger age-group and stated categorically that they had to change the old attitude because in a number of cases they had observed that a mother-in-law unnecessarily harassed her daughter-in-law. The response to the question as to what respondents themselves did/would do when confronted/would confront such a situation, was on the same pattern as mentioned above.

Respondents were also asked to react to a few statements provided to them, with a view to gathering information regarding mother-in-law and daughter-in-law relationship in general. They were mostly of the view that daughters-in-law would generally adopt a defiant attitude towards their mothers-in-law and a growing tendency, especially in the urban areas, was that the former would rarely like to stay with the latter.

To sum up: First, living separately from one's mother, responsibilities of one's nuclear units, and the unaccommodating nature of mother seem to affect son's loyalty towards mother adversely, though the traditional value of man being closer to mother than to wife continues to exist to a large extent. Secondly, in spite of the persistence of this bond loyalty the present day mother-in-law does not enjoy the same authoritative position vis-a-vis her daughter-in-law, as was the practice earlier. Thirdly, the chances of strain in the relations between the two are enchanced when they live together. Finally, daughters-in-law adopted a defiant attitude towards their mothers-in-law and prefer to stay in a separate household than with her. This can finally lead to their residential separation.

IV

Brother-Brother Relationship

The last relationship we shall be dealing with is the one between brothers which is significant from the point of view of a fraternal joint family. In a Hindu family, this relationship is "ranked next in importance to that of father and son" (Levy, quoted by Ross, 1961: 162). The traditional hierarchical position of brothers in a family was determined by age. "The authority of brothers followed their age sequence, with the eldest brother holding a particularly powerful position" (Ross, 1961 : 108).

Not only after father's death, even during his life time, the eldest son by virtue of his age enjoyed authoritative position over his siblings, though the over-all authority rested with father. If father wanted to delegate authority during his life because of ill health or old age, he would do so in favour of the eldest son, who in return, was expected to look after the interests of his younger brothers and sisters, who were expected to recognise his authority without any hesitation. Commenting on the authority pattern between brothers, Mandelbaum (1972: 39) writes:"Among brothers, authority rests with the elder. Some of the same respectful compliance that a son gives to his father, a younger brother should give, in formal terms at least, to his elder brother. When an eldest brother succeeds as head of the joint family, his younger brothers, and their wives and children, are supposed to give him the kind of allegiance and obedience that the father commanded".

The authority of the elder brother continued to be powerful even after separation because brothers were not 'separated from each other's authority' (Ross, 1961: 109). The execution of authority by the elder brother and acceptance of his authority by the younger(s) must have been comparatively easy when the brothers lived together or even in separate households but in near vicinity. It suited them very well because "living in villages, they had common problems and interests to bind them together..."(Ross, 1961: 162). The elder brother wielded authority not only because of tradition but also because "he passed through the usual experiences of life before his younger siblings, he was in a position to lead and guide them" (Ross, 1961: 108). But with the changing socio-economic scene this pattern changed. On account of growing industrialisation the migration of younger generation from rural to urban areas and the mobility of city dwellers from one place to another increased considerably. This brought about bifurcation in households. A decline in the traditional authority pattern would be "inevitable when brothers live in nuclear households, (and) each lives his own life and there is no common pattern to which all brothers need to conform" (Dhirendra Narain, 1970: 469).

It is with this background in mind that we shall be dealing with the inter-personal relations between brothers focussing on the following aspects of their relationship.

i. Existing authority pattern between brothers, by studying (a) the respondent vis-a-vis his elder brother, and (b) the respondent vis-s-vis his younger brother (only married and earning younger brothers would be considered). The authority pattern will be determined by the extent to which the respondents comply with the instructions issued or advice given by their elder brothers and the extent to which their instructions are being complied with by their younger brothers.
ii. Whether or not age difference among brothers continues to be recognized as a mark of respect, and
iii. Whether or not the relations between brothers, in general, and respondents and their brothers in particular are cordial.

To avoid any hypothetical answer only those respondents who had elder and/or younger brother(s) either living with them, living separately or living with the parents were considered.

Respondents vis-a-vis their elder brother(s)

Out of the total sample workers only 179[6] (169 in nuclear households and 10 in joint households) had elder brothers. Of these, twenty one respondents reported that their elder brothers did not issue any instructions to them because their brothers thought them responsible enough to deal with different issues concerning the family and related affairs independently. These respondents belonged to the elderly age-group. Ten respondents were not given any instructions by their elder brothers as the relations between the two were not cordial. Some of them were not even on talking terms. Elder brothers of the remaining 148 respondents, of course, counselled them on various occasions either on asking or of their own. All these respondents receiving instructions from their elder brother were asked whether they complied with these instructions.

Table 5.6 shows that the traditional norm predominates but the deviations are not non-existent: More than one-fifth (21.6%) of the respondents reported that they complied with the instructions only occasionally, followed by about 7% who did so rarely. Most of the respondents of these two categories said that their elder brothers lived in villages and wanted them to lead their life according to their

TABLE 5.6: **Extent of Compliance with Elder Brothers' Instructions**

S. No.	Extent of compliance	Respondent vis-a-vis elder brother(s)		Younger brother vis-a-vis the Respondent	
		No. of Respondents	Percentage	No. of Respondents	Percentage
1.	Always	104	70.2	40	51.2
2.	Occasionally	32	21.6	21	26.9
3.	Rarely	10	6.7	10	12.8
4.	Never	2	1.5	7	9.1
	Total	148	100.0	78	100.0

(elder brother's) instructions, which they felt was very difficult. One of the respondents, for instance, reported that his elder brother did not like his going to a movie. Another respondent's elder brother did not want him to participate in the union activities of the Mill, he violated his instructions because he thought that worker's strength lay in the union. Only the remaining two respondents (1.5%) never complied with their instructions. No significant variations were found on the basis of variables, such as age, education, duration of stay.

Respondents vis-a-vis younger brother(s)

Only 78 respondents[7] have been studied in relation to their younger brothers. They were asked if their younger brother(s) complied with their instructions or advice. As table 5.6 indicates, a little more than half of the respondents (51.2%) reported that their younger brothers always complied with their instructions, while in the case of more than one-fourth (26.9%) compliance was only occasional. About 13% of the respondents reported that their younger brothers rarely followed their instructions or advice while in the case of the remaining 9% younger brothers paid no heed to the instructions of their elder brothers (the respondents). When asked why they told their brothers to do or not to do certain things, they said that they could not ignore their responsibilities as elder brothers.

A comparison of the two positions in the table--respondent vis-a-vis his elder brother(s) and respondent vis-a-vis his younger brother--clearly indicates a deviation from the traditional pattern. Incidentally, respondents, especially of the elderly age-groups, were on the whole very critical of the younger generation and felt that with changing times the younger generation was becoming more and more indifferent towards their elders.

Age as a mark of respect or authority

Second part of enquiry deals with finding whether age difference between brothers continues to be a mark of respect and authority. Most of the respondents reported that the importance of difference in age was diminishing. When asked about their private behaviour most of them apparently attached importance to the age factor. But a look into the pattern of functional relationships in Chapter IV and the compliance with elder brothers' instructions and advice definitely indicates that the age difference remains only a formal sign of status differentiation. The separation pattern elaborately explained in the preceding chapter also confirmed that age difference no longer remains an important consideration for the relationship between brothers.

General Observation of Respondents

Our sample for the study of relationship between brothers was considerably reduced, because all the respondents did not have brothers. Besides, some had only elder or younger brothers. Even this small sample lacked uniformity. We had, therefore, to supplement this part of our study with the general observations of the respondents in regard to the nature of relationship that exists between brothers these days.

The respondents reported that cordiality between brothers lasted only till the parents were alive. After their death, particularly the male parent, and when the brothers are employed, the relations between them get strained either due to quarrels between their wives or difference on sharing the household expenditures. The general impression of the respondents was that brothers remained cordial till there was no big income differential between them. After establishing their separate nuclear units they establish nuclear families. Cordiality is maintained only to the extent of paying reciprocal visits and help is exchanged on the principle of mutual benefit. Respondents of the elderly age-group expressed their disgust over the changing pattern of relationships which they had observed around them. Occupational diversity, differences in income levels and urban living have made people individualistic, and rarely do brothers do anything worthwhile for each other.

A comparison of our findings with the traditional pattern brings out the deviations in inter-personal relations. Neither father over his son, nor husband over his wife, nor elder brother over his younger brother, nor even mother-in-law over her daughter-in-law enjoys the traditional authority. Another noteworthy feature is that the authority pattern even in the joint households which have been designated as joint families on the basis of some concrete characteristics of joint family is changing. Also, there is a difference between the behaviour patterns of migrant and native: migrant are more attached to the traditional norms than native. If we assume that the authority pattern in its traditional form had any role to play in the sustenance of the joint family he dwindling authority of elder and the changing pattern of relatic ship between husband and wife is certainly going to weaken it.

NOTES

1. Out of 394 respondents 22 had lost their father at an early age and, therefore, were not in a position to reply the question.
2. Like stories of Rama, Shrawan Kumar, etc.
3. Like running away from home or committing suicide by throwing themselves under running trains.
4. Discussed elaborately in Chapter VII.
5. For details on this aspect, see Chapter VI.
6. The number of respondents having elder brothers is different here when compared with the respondents studied in relation to elder brothers in section (D) dealing with 'seeking advice and approval of elders' in Chapter IV. There we considered only those respondents who have elder rbothers but no parents but here we shall deal with all the respondents having elder brother(s), irrespective of whether their parents are alive or not.
7. Having younger brother(s).

SIX

Institution of Marriage

Marriage is considered by Hindus as a necessary "religious and a social duty" (Goode, 1963: 208). Pointing out its importance, Karve (1965: 130) observes: "... if a woman dies a spinster a marriage ceremony is performed with the corpse and the woman is then cremated with the honour due to a married woman. There is a greater freedom for man, but if a man who has gone through the initiation ceremony dies without marrying, he is supposed to be a ghost". Emphasising the importance of marriage for women, Shah (1975: 293) quotes a story from the Mahabharata in which "we are told that it was impossible for a lady who remained single to gain the ultimate bliss as long as she was not sanctified by marriage ties". This makes marriage a very important institution in our social set-up.

Almost all the sociologists maintain that the institution of marriage and the form in which it has been maintained has played a great role in the continuity of the joint family system in India. We have, therefore, analysed the opinions of the respondents on the aspects of the institution of marriage to ascertain the future of the joint family system. A comparative study of the past practice and the present position as also the opinion of the respondents regarding the different characteristics of the institution of marriage would help in predicting the likely changes in the joint family.

The major aspects of the institution of marriage which we have chosen for our study are based largely on Gore (1968: 198):

1. Age at marriage,
2. Process of mate selection,and
3. Prohibition of widow remarriage.

The opinion of the respondents on these aspects has been analysed under (i) different age-groups of the respondents, and (ii) their residential background, i.e., whether they are native or migrant.

1. **Age at Marriage**

The stability of the joint family depended largely on the age-at-marriage. Though marriageable age has been varying for both men and women, from time to time, and from region to region, child marriage has been a prevalent practice in India since 200 B.C. The origin of child marriage may be traced in social customs prescribed by Smritis. Mireille Abeille (1955: 41-52) observes: "All the Smritis after (Manu) urged the marrying of girls before puberty". Shah (1975: 296-97) notes that "The later Smritis show five categories of marriageable girls, namely, nagnika (naked), gauri (eight year old), rohini (nine year old), Kanya (ten year old), and rajasvala (one who has reached puberty). Nagnika was regarded as the best for marriage". The continuity of the practice is confirmed by the Census report of 1961 according to which 1,733,000 males and 4,426,000 females were married between the ages of ten and fourteen during 1951-61.[1] Until recently, a girl "was supposed to marry before she attained puberty" (Ross, 1961: 246). It was ordinarily considered sinful if parents did not marry off their daughters at pre-puberty stage, possibly because they would not earn the gains of a 'kanya dan' after that a girl was treated as a 'kanya' before she attained puberty. We can say almost the same for boys. According to Ghurye (1954: 42-50),"...from 1860 to 1890, for example, the 'proper' age-at-marriage was 8 for girls and 12 for boys". In the opinion of Ross (1961: 246), a girl was to be married "before she could lose her virginity or be suspected of having lost it". Marriage at an early age was a common practice among the Hindus.

The main objective behind such a practice seems to have been the intention of strengthening the joint family by (a) preventing the possibility of opposition from spouses who are shifted from her father's family to husband's family, and (b) making them financially dependent on the elders of the family. According to Kapadia (quoted by Ross, 1961: 246), early marriage was intended to keep the woman under the domination of the elders of the husband's family. This was possibly easier when girls were married before they attained the age at which they could question the authority of their elders. According to Ross (1961: 48), "One advantage of child marriage was that the bride was young enough to learn how to fit into the new strange household. Part of her training for her future adult responsibility was thus undertaken by her mother-in-law". Early marriage of a girl "would ensure her loyalties" to her in-laws, and also "A girl would be bound by ties of companionship to the members of her husband's family long before she started her life as the wife of a person" (Karve, 1965: 73). This objective could be fulfilled only when a girl, at the time of her marriage, was young, innocent and illiterate. Gore (1968: 19) too observes that "The young girl was a child and, therefore, amenable to advice and admonition". Mendalbaum (1948: 101) also states "...the young bride enters a household group in which she becomes the most subordinate member, owning immediate and implicit obedience to her mother-in-law". Pointing out its importance from the psychological point of view, Williams (quoted by Prabhu, 1963: 184) says "...if married early, the nature of each is still plastic, and there is a greater possibility of congeniality, than later when the characteristic attitudes have become fixed".

Another important purpose behind the early marriage of boys and girls was to burden them with marital responsibilities before they could develop their own individuality and authority: "youngsters were married early enough to ensure that they could not acquire any resources with which to oppose adult decisions. The joint family, in turn, offered an organisation which could absorb a young couple who could not yet make their own living" (Goode, 1963: 208).

Besides, there were other arrangements in the household which were helpful in checking the "development of an intensely emotional relationship between husband and wife" (Gore, 1968: 7). Such a relationship was considered a threat to the joint family, and was sought to be "eliminated by the insistence upon segregating sexes within the household both before and after marriage" (Goode, 1963: 240). Child marriage, on the one hand, and segregation of sexes on the other, worked together to prevent the development of emotional attachment between wife and husband. Thus, conjugal relationship which could be a threat to joint family was "subordinate(d) to the requirements of the larger system" (Gore, 1968: 7; Vatuk, 1972; 113). Given the social customs, a young wife had to fit into the new pattern with no chance of asserting her own individuality. The daughters-in-law till the time of attaining adulthood were completely integrated in the joint family and had no courage to oppose their elders. Child marriages, therefore, were a big help in the stability and continuity of the joint family.

But the general attitude towards child marriage and early marriage has changed a great deal because of (i) the efforts made by social reformers to awaken the people against the evils of child marriage, (ii) the enactment of legislations against early marriage, and (iii) people's own realisation of the drawbacks of early marriage. These reasons have, however, influenced the attitude of urban populace more than that of rural masses. Now, since industrialisation is attracting rural population to the cities and migration is taking place at a fast rate, it is quite likely that the attitude of the rural migrants towards marriageable age would change under the environmental influence of the urban society. If the attitude of the rural migrants towards marriageable age changes, and if, as a result of it, the migrants decide to arrange the marriage of their children at a relatively higher age, it may well be expected to affect the joint family system. It is in view of this that an attempt has been made here to find out the change in the attitude, if any, of both migrant and native respondents[2] and also to see how such a change is likely to affect the Institution in future.

For this purpose, we compared the age-at-marriage of the respondent himself and the age at which he would like his children to get married. A substantial difference in the two ages would be taken as an indicator of the changing trend. It is expected that a rise in the age-at-marriage of both girls and boys would give them an opportunity to assert themselves, and also that they may not as readily accept the subordinate position as was accorded to them earlier. Along with it, greater mobility offered by industrialisation would give a chance to the newly-married couples to establish a separate household. This can result in a closer intimacy between husband and wife and the superiority of conjugal relations over the consanguineal relations.

Respondents' Age at Marriage

Our study summed up in table 6.1 supports the general upward trend in the age-at-marriage in India. Considering marriage at or below the age of 16 years as child marriage, the percentage of respondents having been married at or below the age of 16 years as child marriage, the percentage of respondents having been married at or below this age showed an upward trend from about 21% for the youngest generation of workers (18-35 years) to 91.3% in the case of oldest generation (46-60 years). Besides, about 80% of the respondents in the age group 18-35 years were married at or above the age of 17 years. This is positive indication towards rise in the age-at-marriage. It is noteworthy that the older the respondent the lower the age at which he had married and vice versa.

TABLE 6.1 : **Respondents' Age-at-marriage by Age-groups**

Sl. No.	Age group	Respondents' Age-at-marriage								Total
		14-16 yrs		17-19 yrs		20-22 yrs		23-25 yrs		
		No.	%*	No.	%*	No.	%*	No.	%*	
1		2	3	4	5	6	7	8	9	10
1.	18-35	39	20.7	61	32.3	72	38.0	17	9.0	189
2.	36-45	90	79.6	23	20.4	-	-	-	-	113
3.	46-60	84	91.3	8	8.7	-	-	-	-	92
	Total	213	54.0	92	23.6	72	18.2	17	4.2	394

* Percentages refer to the number of respondents in each age-group (col.10).

Age of Respondents and Opinion on Marriageable Age

While earlier people generally preferred pre-puberty age for the marriage of their daughters, none of the respondents, as is clear from table 6.2(A), irrespective of their age, caste, educational standards or rural or urban background was prepared to see his daughter married before she attained the age of 14. 67.3% reported that they would like to celebrate the marriage of their daughters after they were 17. This included 5.5% respondents who said that they would not mind getting their daughters married even after they were 20 years old. Only the remaining 32.7% preferred 14-16 years as a suitable age for the marriage of their daughters. Respondents of the last category mentioned that they preferred lower age for their daughters' marriage mainly because they wanted to get rid of their parental responsibilities before their retirement. Another reason they gave for their preference was that for girls of higher age one had to find an earning boy who had to be paid a bigger dowry. Thus we see that the younger the generation, the higher the preferred age-at-marriage for daughters. There seems to be a direct relationship between the age of the respondent and the preferred age for marriage of their children. This conclusion is similar to Mandelbaum's (1972: 648) that "The age of girls in most parts of India is steadily and significantly rising".

TABLE 6.2 (A) : **Respondents' Age-wise preference for Marriageable age**
(For Girls)

S.No.	Respondents' Age-group	Preferred age-at-marriage 14-16 yrs	17-19 yrs	20-22 yrs	Total
1.	18-35	23 (12.2)	146 (77.2)	20 (10.6)	189 (100.0)
2.	36-45	45 (39.8)	66 (58.4)	2 (1.8)	113 (100.0)
3.	46-60	61 (66.3)	31 (33.7)	- (-)	92 (100.0)
	Total	129 (32.7)	243 (61.8)	22 (5.5)	394 (100.0)

TABLE 6.2 (B)

(For Boys)

S.No.	Respondents' Age-group	14-16 yrs	17-19 yrs	20-22 yrs	Total
1.	18-35	- (-)	57 (30.3)	132 (69.7)	189 (100.0)
2.	36-45	9 (8.1)	26 (22.9)	78 (69.0)	113 (100.0)
3.	46-60	16 (17.5)	23 (25.0)	53 (57.5)	92 (100.0)
	Total	25 (6.4)	106 (26.9)	263 (66.7)	394 (100.0)

The rising trend in the age-at-marriage of girls is equally true of boys. Table 6.2(B) shows that 66.7% respondents prefer 20-22 years of age for their sons' marriage while those who prefer 17-19 years of age account for 26.9%. Respondents of these two categories who account for 26.9% of the total respondents consider 17 years or more (but not exceeding 22 years) as the suitable age for the marriage of boys. Only 6.4% prefer 14-16 years of age for their sons' marriage: They want to fulfil their parental duty, as in the case of girls, as early as possible (obviously not before 14 or 15 years of their sons' age.)

Another significant conclusion which can be drawn from the table is that the younger the age of the respondent the higher the preferred age for his son's marriage. About 70% of the respondents belonging to the age group 18-35 years prefer 20-22 years for the marriage of their sons while the corresponding percentage for the oldest generation of the respondents (46-60) is only 57.5%.

Residential Background and Opinion on Marriageable Age

Analysis of opinions on marriageable age on the basis of residential background of the respondents is also quite revealing. No native respondent, probably on account of urban influence, is in favour of getting his daughter(s) married at an early age, i.e., below 16 years. Of native respondents, 73% reported that with changing times daughter(s) could be married only when they were mature enough to shoulder family/household responsibilities. Marriageable age for girls, according to them, should not be less than 16 years. Some of the native respondents (27%) even preferred a still higher age (20-22 years). All of them favoured the complete eradication of the custom of child marriage. This finding is similar to that of Kapadia (1966: 165); he found in his study that the model age specified for marriage by his teacher respondents was 16-18 years for girls.

The opinion of migrant respondents on this question is slightly different from that of native ones. None of the native respondents favoured 14-16 years as the minimum marriageable age for their daughters. On the contrary out of 331 migrant respondents about 39% showed their inclination for getting their daughters married between 14 and 16 years. The remaining 61% preferred 17 years or more. The most significant point to be noted here is that even the migrant respondents who have no academic attainments did not favour pre-puberty marriage although their relatives at village as per their own statement still preferred comparatively lower age for girl's marriage. Almost a similar trend can be perceived in the attitude of respondents regarding the marriageable age of their son(s). A very large majority of native respondents (90.4%) preferred the age of 20 years or more for the marriage of their sons. The corresponding percentage for the migrant respondents is 62.2. In all two-thirds of total respondents considered this age group (i.e., 20-22 years) as the appropriate age for the marriage of boys. Among the native and migrant respondents 9.6% and 30.2% respectively reported having preference for an age group between 17 and 19 years. Only 7.6% migrant respondents reported having preference for 14-16 years of age for their son's marriage, while no native respondent preferred this age group. It is noteworthy that native respondents, by and large, preferred higher marriageable age both for boys and girls than their migrant counterparts.

According to our findings migration to the city seems to have affected the attitude of migrant respondents in regard to marriageable age. Gore (1968: 201) has also found that "The urban groups tend to specify a higher age for boys as well as girls" for their marriage. Whatever the reason for this, there is a definite trend towards a higher marriageable age for both girls and boys. This change is bound to have its impact on the institution of the joint family by affecting it adversely. Marriage at a higher age and migration to the city may lead to the strengthening of conjugal bond and weaken the filial and fraternal loyalty which are central to the joint family (Gore, 1968: 21).

2. Process of Mate Selection

The second characteristic of the traditional institution of marriage amongst Hindus, which has been very helpful in stabilising the joint family system, relates to the process of mate selection. The most important considerations involved in the process of mate selection and relevant to the purpose of the present study are: (a) Field of Selection and (b) Authority of Selection.

Field of Selection

Every society has certain restrictions relating to the selection of mate by its members which determine the course of mate selection: "There is no known society which does not restrict marriage relations by some kind of exogamic or endogamic rules" (Prabhu, 1963: 157). But, as Shah (1975: 288) observes, "In different societies, values, norms, and rules differ as to who shall or shall not marry whom". The basic norm governing the process of mate selection amongst Hindus was that one had normally to marry within one's caste. Although inter-caste marriages were not completely unknown, they invited punishment from society: "Until recently breaches of caste endogamy were punished by excommunication from the caste" (Kapadia, 1966: 118). That is why endogamy was a general rule.

Endogamous marriages were of immense help in the stability of the joint family. For, each caste had uniform traditions which the caste members were obliged to follow. The bride and the groom were reared according to common traditions, which were internalised in their personalities. This reduced the possibilities of friction between a woman and her in-laws and her adjustment to the changed situation was almost smooth due to similar, if not identical, cultural background: "The bride's obedience to the mother-in-law becomes easier since the latter has also been brought up in the same traditions..." (Gore, 1968: 19).

But there are reasons to believe that social rigidities regarding exogamous marriages are gradually relaxing. First, laws have been enacted from time to time to change this custom. The Special Marriage Act of 1872 allowed a man to contract legal marriage with a person not belonging to his own endogamous group. Besides, the Hindus Marriages Validity Act (1949) provides that "no marriage between Hindus shall be deemed to be invalid or even to have been invalid by reason only of the fact that the parties thereto belonged to different religions, castes, sub-castes or sects". In addition to these, many other factors have contributed to the decline in endogamous marriages: "(i) the opportunities provided to young men and women to get together in co-educational schools and mixed clubs and (ii) mixed employment in factories, schools, commercial firms and Government offices" (Kapadia, 1966: 123). Enlarging on these, Shah

(1975: 299) points out that "Several multidirectional forces arising out of the social reform movement, industrialisation, urbanisation, legislations, and socio-educational advancement have brought about changes in the Hindu practice of mate selection during the twentieth century".

Such a trend in favour of exogamous marriage would definitely widen the field of selection and promote intercaste marriages. This trend would no doubt manifest itself predominantly among the urban population, but rural population can hardly be assumed to remain unaffected by the change towards exogamous marriage. Growing industrialisation, availability of jobs in the cities, migration from rural to urban areas, and temporary or permanent settlement in the urban areas, shall bring at least a section of rural population under the influence of the social customs prevailing in the urban areas. This may well be supposed to bring a change in life-style of migrant population ultimately leading to further relaxation in the rigidities regarding exogamous marriage. It would bring together people--daughters-in-law and mothers-in-law--of diverse backgrounds amongst whom adjustment would be comparatively difficult. This would ultimately lead to the instability of the joint family.

In order to find out if there is really any change in the attitude of our respondents towards the custom of caste endogamy, we made enquiries regarding (i) whether the norm of caste endogamy has been followed when the respondents were married, (ii) whether they would follow this practice in case of their children's marriage, (iii) whether they would allow their children to marry outside their caste, and (iv) whether they would accept their son and his wife in the family if he married a woman of some other caste.

Respondents' Marriage and the Norm of Caste Endogamy

On enquiry we found that 390 respondents out of 394 were married within their caste; only 4 belonging to younger generation had married outside their caste. Incidentally all of them belonged to Delhi, had passed secondary examinations and had separated from their parents either at the insistence of their parents or of their own will.

TABLE 6.3: **Respondents' opinion on Inter-caste Marriage by Age-groups**

S.No.	Respondents' Age-group	Only within caste No.	%*	May be outside caste No.	%*	Total
	1	2	3	4	5	6
1.	18-35	108	57.1	81	42.9	189
2.	36-45	94	83.1	19	16.9	113
3.	46-60	87	94.5	5	5.5	92
	Total	289	73.3	105	26.7	394

* Percentages refer to the number of respondents in each age-group (col. 6)

Age of Respondents and opinion on Inter-caste Marriage

Nearly three-fourths of the respondents (73.3%) favoured caste endogamy (Table 6.3). Majority of the respondents of this category could not specifically state their reaction to inter-caste marriage by their children. Some of them (22), stated emphatically that they would turn the errant out of their family, because it would create many social problems for all other members of the family; it would cause a fall in social prestige and create problems in the marriage of other children. Only the remaining 26.7% reported that they would not mind getting their children married outside their caste[3]. Gore's study of Agarwals (1968: 206) confirms our findings: "89% were not in favour of intercaste or inter-subcaste marriages".

Thus it is clear that social rigidity in regard to endogamy has considerably relaxed; this would certainly contribute towards instability in the institution of the joint family.

Majority of the respondents in all the three categories were in favour of endogamous marriages. The most interesting feature was that the respondents who did not mind getting their children married outside their caste belonged to the younger age group (18-35). The percentage of such respondents was minimum--(5.5%) in the older age group (46-60). A comparison of the three categories of respondents' age and their opinion on inter-caste marriage reveals that the younger generation has a liberal attitude towards inter-caste marriage, which may weaken the stability of the joint family considerably.

Residential Background and the opinion on inter-caste marriage

So far as the preferences of native and migrant respondents are concerned, a little more than two-thirds (69.8%) of native were willing to allow their children to marry outside their caste: the percentage of migrant respondents was only 18.5. This shows that people with a rural background are still in favour of endogamy. Nevertheless, with growing industrialisation leading to the migration of people from rural to urban areas, the winds of change can spread faster than normally expected. The study made by Kapadia (1966: 119) substantiates the fact that social rigidities regarding endogamous marriages are weakening and exogamous marriages are gradually becoming popular.

Authority of Selection

The second consideration in the process of mate selection is the authority of mate selection, i.e., who has the authority of selecting mates--parents, relatives or the parties concerned? Among Hindus the authority of selecting spouses rested with the elders, possibly because the children to be married were too young to select mates for themselves: "In the traditional joint family parents were morally obliged to find mates for their children and the children to accept their choice" (Ross; 1961: 251). Shah (1975: 298) confirms it and further states that "The theory of love in mate selection has practically no chance in the traditional Hindu society". However, it does not mean that love marriage or marriage by choice was not known: "Manu did recognise mate selection by mutual choice, but he placed it far down on his list of preferences, and looked on it as highly undesirable" (Ross, 1961: 251). In the general practice, therefore, selection of spouse was the authority of elders, and the individuals involved had hardly any say in the selection of their marriage partners. Although eight different forms of marriages were recognised amongst Hindus in traditional India yet in no form, according to Goode (1963: 208), "the bride or groom [had] any real voice in the decision".

Arranged marriages are said to have been a big help in the perpetuation of the joint family mostly because they limited the development of prior loyalty between husband and wife and helped subordinating conjugal bond to the consanguineal relations. This proved a powerful stabilising factor in the joint family: "The love and affection between spouses, which might break the joint unit into nuclear families, does not play a major role, since marriages are arranged before a love relationship can develop" (Goode, 1963: 240).

Since the custom of child marriage is gradually disappearing and boys and girls are married at a relatively higher age, they are not expected to blindly accept the choice made by their elders. They may demand freedom and right to choose their own partners: "...in mate choice...there is a movement in the direction of giving greater freedom to the young" (Goode, 1963: 207-08). Ross (1961: 253) confirms it:"...young people themselves tend to select the person they want to marry, and ask their parents' approval of their choice." Under changing social conditions, this trend is bound to gain favour among the people of all castes and creed. And, if man and woman take active interest in mate selection, it might give supremacy to conjugal intimacy over consanguineal intimacy. This change will certainly affect the stability of the joint family.

To find out whether there has been any change in the authority regarding the selection of spouse in the case of industrial workers, we elicited information from the respondents on two points: (i) whether mates for them were selected with or without consulting them, or their consent was taken, or whether they were given a free choice for doing so, and (ii) would they consult their children, get their consent, or give them full freedom in selecting their spouses?

Pattern of Mate Selection followed in case of the Respondents

Table 6.4 reveals that a vast majority of respondents (88.3%) were not at all consulted in the selection of their mates: selection in their case was done on the traditional pattern. Only 10.6% respondents reported that their consent was taken, though a number of them reported that the selection had already been made by the elders of the family or other relatives, and asking for their consent was only a formality. Full freedom in mate selection was enjoyed only by the remaining negligible percentage (1.1).

TABLE 6.4: Pattern of Mate Selection followed in case of Respondents by Age group

Sl. No.	Respondents, Age group	Married without consultation	Married with consent	Got free choice	Total
	1	2	3	4	5
1.	18-35	155 (82.0)	30 (15.8)	4 (2.2)	189 (100.0)
2.	36-45	101 (89.3)	12 (10.7)	- (-)	113 (100.0)
3.	46-60	92 (100.0)	- (-)	- (-)	92 (100.0)
	Total	348 (88.3)	42 (10.6)	4 (1.1)	394 (100.0)

Age of the Respondents and the Pattern of Mate-Selection followed

A comparison of responses on the basis of age group of respondents reveals some very interesting trends. Table 6.4 shows that the percentage of those who were married without being consulted is minimum (82.0) among the respondents belonging to the youngest age-group (18-35). It increases to 89.3% and 100% in the case of respondents belonging to the age-groups 36-45 and 46-60 years of age respectively. The obvious conclusion is that the older the category of respondents the more is the percentage of those who were not at all consulted in the selection of their spouse and vice versa. The gradual deviation from the traditional norm is, therefore, evident. Secondly, respondents whose consent was taken mostly belong to the younger age groups. This gives another indication of the gradual breaking away from the traditional pattern of mate-selection. Lastly, those who were given free choice in their mate selection belong to the youngest age group. Though their percentage (2.2) is not significant, it does indicate that even among industrial workers, some have had complete freedom in the selection of their spouses.

The table on the whole suggests a great deal of association between the age of the respondents and the extent of freedom enjoyed by them in this regard. If this trend continues, one can visualise that the coming generations are bound to enjoy more freedom in mate selection; this will affect the institution of the joint family adversely.

Residential Background and the Pattern of the Mate Selection followed

A comparison between the responses of migrant and native respondents reveals that as many as 98.4% migrants reported not having been consulted at all; in native it was only about 35%. Mates for 60.3% native respondents were selected with their consent, while only a negligible (1.2%) was consulted among migrants. Of the remaining 4 respondents who reported to have enjoyed full freedom in mate selection, 3 belonged to Delhi and the other one was a migrant. On the whole, the native respondents have had a fairly larger degree of freedom in mate selection than their migrant counterparts.

Age of the Respondent and readiness to allow freedom of Mate Selection

A vast majority (76.7%) of respondents (Table 6.5A) belonging to the age group 18-35 years expressed their willingness to consult and/or take the consent of their daughter(s) in selecting a match for them. The corresponding percentage for boys is still higher i.e., 84.6 (Table 6.5B). This percentage goes down drastically in the case of respondents of the middle age group and the older generation. Similarly, the proportion of respondents who would neither consult nor take the consent of their children increased as one moved from the young generation to older one. Although the percentage of respondents who expressed their willingness to grant full freedom of choice to their children--within caste or community--is very low, i.e., 4.4% in case of girls and 9.5 in case of boys, it marks a definite change in the attitude towards the mode of selection of spouses. Parents of young generation are willing to share the authority of mate selection with their children. Hemalatha Acharya (1974: 187) is quite close to our findings: "There is more freedom today in the choice of mates, though mostly within castes".

TABLE 6.5(A): **Respondents' readiness to allow freedom of Mate Selection by Age Group** (For Girls)

Sl. No.	Respondents' Age group	Extent of freedom			Total
		Not to be consulted at all	Consent to be taken	Full freedom	
	1	2	3	4	5
1.	18-35	27 (14.2)	145 (76.7)	17 (9.1)	189 (100.0)
2.	36-45	92 (81.4)	21 (18.6)	- (-)	113 (100.0)
3.	46-60	85 (92.4)	7 (7.6)	- (-)	92 (100.0)
	Total	204 (51.7)	173 (43.9)	17 (4.4)	394 (100.0)

TABLE 6.5(B): **Respondents' readiness to allow freedom of Mate Selection by Age Group** (For Boys)

S.No.	Respondents Age group	Extent of Freedom			Total
		Not to be consulted	Consent to be taken	Full freedom	
	1	2	3	4	5
1.	18-35	- (-)	160 (84.6)	29 (15.4)	189 (100.0)
2.	36-45	6 (5.3)	99 (87.6)	8 (7.1)	113 (100.0)
3.	46-60	42 (45.7)	50 (54.3)	- (-)	92 (100.0)
	Total	48 (12.1)	309 (78.4)	37 (9.5)	394 (100.0)

In all 4.4% have at least an intention to do so in the case of their daughters, and 9.5% in the case of sons. If this category is considered alongwith those having desire to part with the authority of mate selection in favour of their children, the proportion of respondents having expressed their intention to adopt a liberal attitude in mate selection rises further: about 48% in the case of girls and 88% in the case of boys.

The trend can further be substantiated by the fact that, in all, only about 12% (Table 6.4) respondents were either consulted or given full freedom in their mate selection whereas 88% (Table 6.5 B) were willing to either consult or give full freedom to their sons in the selection of their spouses.

Residential Background and readiness to allow freedom of Mate Selection

That there is a good deal of likelihood of change in authority in mate selection in favour of parties concerned becomes more obvious in the study of respondents' opinion based on their residential background. The spouses for about 35% of native respondents were chosen without consulting them, 60.3% were consulted and 4.8% were given free choice, of course, within caste. So far as the question of respondents' readiness to allow freedom of mate selection is concerned, only 6.3% native respondents feel that it is not necessary to consult or take consent of boys in the selection of their spouses. Incidentally, they are of the opinion that it is the obligation of the parents to get brides for their sons, otherwise they would be failing in their duty. The remaining 94% native respondents think it desirable to take the consent of their boys or to give them freedom to choose their own spouses. Those who think it is enough if they took their consent account for about 70% of native respondents. Those who would like to give full freedom in the selection of spouses account for about 24% whereas only about 5% native respondents had enjoyed this freedom.

What is much more important and noteworthy is the reported change in the attitude of the respondents towards the authority of selection. 98.4% migrant were not at all consulted in the selection of their spouses; only 1.2% were perfunctorily asked for their opinion.

Contrasted with these the majority of migrant respondents is now in favour of sharing the authority of spouse selection with the boys. Of the total migrant respondents, 80% feel it desirable to consult and get the consent of boys in the selection of their spouses whereas 6.7% expressed the desire to give up this traditional authority in favour of boys. On the basis of this, one can safely say that there is a definite likelihood of change in the authority of the selection of spouses.

So far as the question of sharing of authority of spouse selection in the case of girls is concerned, unfortunately no comparable data regarding the extent of freedom given to girls (particularly respondents' wives and sisters) in the selection of the spouses could be obtained from the respondents. Among the native respondents, the majority (57.3%) were in favour of consulting or taking consent of girls, while 36.4% did not feel it necessary. What is significant is that 41.3% migrant also expressed their willingness to get the consent of their daughters in the selection of their husbands, though the majority (54.7%) still does not favour it. But, compared with the earlier practice of 'no consultation or consent at all', even this percentage reveals a remarkable change in the attitude of migrant respondents in regard to the authority of mate selection. Kurian (1961: 20) also feels that "Marriage is no longer a transaction between two families, but the individual parties concerned are consulted and their approval is necessary..."

It may be inferred from the foregoing discussion that, in future, most of the respondents would like to consult or take consent of their children in the selection of their spouses. Our findings distinctly show a shift from the traditional pattern i.e., concerned parties (boys and girls) not being consulted at all, towards a relatively less rigid system in which majority of parents would seek the opinion of their children, although giving total authority to their children still remains a remote possibility. With the freedom that they have already acquired, girls and boys will have more say and would like to have more authority in mate selection. This will affect the over-all authority pattern of elder members of the family; conjugal bonds will become strong and filial and fraternal bonds will weaken. This shift in bond loyalties will weaken the solidarity of the joint families. This certainly does not augur well for the continuation of the joint family system.

3. Widow Remarriage

Yet another characteristic of Hindu marriage that is said to have been helpful in the stability of the joint family is the traditional prohibition of widow remarriage[4]. It prevented the possibility of the breaking away of a member (the widow) from one family to the other, and helped in maintaining family bonds, which would otherwise have been severed, especially among the fraternal groups. She was prevented from taking away her children, if any, and her husband's share in the family property. The ensuing discussion shows that the traditional rigidity in the people's attitude towards widow remarriage is changing. We have, therefore, studied here the past practice in this regard and the attitude of our respondents to find out the changes, if any, and their likely impact on the joint family system.

In early days, widow remarriage amongst Hindus was either non-existing or so rare that "no example of widow remarriage [is found] in the older literature" (Karve, 1965: 65). It was, however,not completely unknown: it was relatively prevalent in the non-Brahmin groups but "not without some shadow of social disapproval" (Mandelbaum, 1948: 104). And hence a rare occurrence. Generally, widow remarriage used to take place in cases in which "a man could beget on his brother's widow" (Karve, 1965: 65), because whether she continued to remain a widow or married her deceased husband's brother, she continued to be the part and parcel of the family which she had joined as a bride. This helped in the stability of the joint family. For, she continued to be an obedient daughter-in-law; her children, if any, were looked after by family elders, she continued to remain under the subordination of elders; and the property remained undivided.

This situation changed because of the efforts of social reformers, various organisations, and the Government. The Hindu Widow Remarriage Act of 1856 legalised widow marriage and offsprings of such marriages, and "served to reduce the control that family could have on its members" (Gore, 1968: 54). The Act, thus, affected the traditional authority and control of elders, which was the basis of the traditional joint family. Another legislative measure adopted after Independence, the Hindu Succession Act, 1956, confers on the widow, the daughter and the mother the right to inherit property equally with sons. This Act "is likely to affect the unity of the joint family even further by making individuals belonging to different residential and family groups equal claimants to inheritance" (Gore, 1968: 54). Apart from these legislative measures, other factors such as expansion in education, impact of western thinking, playing of important roles by women in public life, are bound to mould the public mind in favour of widow remarriage.

Respondents' Attitude Towards Widow Remarriage

The opinions of the respondents about widow remarriage have been grouped under three categories: (i) those who are totally against it, (ii) those who favour it conditionally, and (iii) those who favour it unconditionally. More than one-third (37.4%) respondents were against it, 58.8% favoured it conditionally; only 3.8% expressed clear support for it.

The opponents of widow remarriage considered it to be against religion. They also stated that it was very difficult to get a respectable match for widows. Only socially degraded people would accept a widow; this would subject her to humiliation.

Those who expressed conditional support for widow remarriage specified their conditions: the widow should be young, issueless, and without any means of support. Incidentally, widow marriages which are taking place in our society fulfill such conditions. Those who favour widow remarriage do so on ideological grounds; for reasons of equality between sexes: if a widower can remarry, widow too should be permitted to remarry. Discrimination on this point is unjust. Some of them also mentioned that the prohibition of widow remarriage is not only a curse but potentially dangerous: widows can go astray because of their physiological and economic compulsions.

Respondents favouring widow remarriage conditionally or unconditionally constitute 62.6% of the total. This is slightly lower than the findings of Gore (1968: 216) where 82% of the respondents favoured the idea. Nevertheless, the tilt towards widow remarriage is conspicuous.

Respondents' Age and Attitude Towards Widow Remarriage

There is a considerable variation in responses in the attitude to widow remarriage on the basis of age groups (Table 6.6). The highest percentage of respondents (87.45%) favouring widow remarriage belong to the youngest age group. In the other two age groups the percentages are about 63 and 12 respectively, indicating that it does not find much favour with the older age groups, re-establishing a very high degree of association between the age of the respondent and his attitude towards widow remarriage. Opposition to the idea is minimum (12.6%) in the youngest age group. It increases to more than 37% in the case of middle-aged, and to more than 88% in the case of the oldest age group (46-60 years). If the trend continues to be the same, one can expect a gradual increase in the number of widow remarriages which will have its impact on the joint family.

TABLE 6.6: **Respondents' Opinion on Widow Remarriage by Age-groups**

S. No.	Respondents' Age Group	In favour No.	In favour %*	Against No.	Against %*	Total
	1	2	3	4	5	6
1.	18-35	165	87.4	24	12.6	189
2.	36-45	71	62.8	42	37.2	113
3.	46-60	11	11.9	81	88.1	92
	Total	247	62.9	147	37.4	394

* Percentages refer to the number of respondents in each age-group (col. 6)

Residential Background and the attitude towards Widow Remarriage

The resident of a metropolitan city is expected to have a broader outlook and, thereby, a less rigid attitude towards traditions than the one who has migrated from a rural area. This proposition is well substantiated by the findings: 92% of native respondents were in favour of widow remarriage while only 8% were averse to it. Correspondingly, only about 58% migrant respondents favoured the proposition and 42% opposed it. It can be inferred that migrant may also change over to the side of natives after their prolonged exposure to the urban environment. Interestingly, we found a number of migrant respondents condemned their relatives back home for holding on to the custom.

Education and the Attitude towards Widow Remarriage

Since education is a major factor in changing the attitude of the people towards social customs, we also tried to study the respondents' attitude towards the issue of widow remarriage vis-a-vis their educational background. Table 6.7 shows that with increase in the level of education, there is an increase in the softening of attitude towards remarriage. This leads to the conclusion that the more educated a respondent, the more is the likelihood of his favouring widow remarriage and vice versa. This finding is similar to that of Gore (1968: 218): "Urban location and higher education were found to be important influences in determining the responses in favour of remarriage."

TABLE 6.7: **Respondents' Opinion on Widow Remarriage by their Educational level**

S. No.	Respondents' Education	In favour No.	In favour %*	Against No.	Against %*	Total
	1	2	3	4	5	6
1.	No Education	5	7.7	62	92.3	67
2.	Primary (1-5)	7	18.0	32	82.0	39
3.	Middle (6-8)	68	36.8	43	63.2	111
4.	Intermediate (8-12)	159	94.0	10	6.0	169
5.	College	8	100.0	-	-	8
	Total	247	62.6	147	37.4	394

* Percentage refer to the number of respondents in each group on the basis of educational level (col. 6).

To sum up this chapter: First of all we discussed the role of child marriage, process of mate selection and prohibition of widow remarriage in the sustenance of the joint family by relying on the evidence of authoritative texts. A thorough analysis of our data has revealed that attitude to all these characteristics of marriage has changed. We have noted: (i) a definite change in age-at-marriage, which is on the increase, (ii) chances of younger generation getting more freedom in the selection of spouse, and (iii) relaxation in the attitude of people towards widow remarriage. All these changes combined together would positively bring husband and wife close to each other and reduce the subordination of the conjugal bond to the filial or fraternal relations. This will ultimately affect the joint family system in future.

With increase in the rate of migration from rural to urban areas and with the expansion of education, people are expected to deviate further from traditional thinking and the norms that governed family ties in the past. And these would expectedly weaken the traditional characteristics of the institution of marriage and consequently the traditional joint family system.

NOTES

1. India 1964: Govt. of India publication, p. 17.
2. All the respondents were asked the question regarding the preferrable age, though all of them did not have a son and/or a daughter.
3. It is noteworthy that this category hardly included any Brahmin.
4. This aspect of the institution of marriage and its relationship to joint family system is however not adequately dealt with by the sociologists. The existing literature on the family yields only conjectural evidence to show how the probibition of widow remarriage was helpful in the stability of the joint family system.

SEVEN

Status of Women

Closely related to the institution of marriage and associated with the functioning of the joint family is the status of woman in society in general and family in particular. In fact, the status of woman, i.e., the liberty she enjoys inside and outside the family and her rights and claims vis-a-vis the menfolk is of a wider significance than the various aspects of the institution of marriage in the functioning of a family. For, while the former determines only the mode of introduction of a female member to the family, the latter determines the pattern of conjugal and consanguineal relationships.

It has been commonly observed that the subordinate status of woman is helpful in maintaining the joint family system because this gives her a subordinate position within the family. She enjoys very little personal freedom, has hardly any decision-making power in regard to internal or external matters of her family, and lives under the control and governance of her superiors and elders who decide matters for her. Her subordinate position gives her hardly any rights or claims; this reduces conflicts and quarrels and prevents separation in the family. Elevation in her status can adversely affect the traditional joint family because an educated woman who marries comparatively at an advanced age after her personality has acquired certain basic traits, has the chances of becoming economically independent; she dislikes purdah system; is emotionally attached to her husband; and does not generally reconcile with the subordinate position which is assigned to her in the joint family in relation to her in-law's, elders and even her husband. For this reason we studied the changes, if any, that have taken place in the status of woman and their likely impact on the joint family.

To do so we assessed the respondents' opinion on the following:

(i) Whether birth of a girl was unwelcome (as it used to be in the past);
(ii) whether education of woman was gaining favour;
(iii) whether women observed purdah in the presence of their elders and outsiders; and
(iv) whether women were allowed to seek employment outside the family.

Such responses helped us to know the present status of woman of industrial workers, and not changes in their status. Therefore, to assess this change we compared these findings (the present status) with the status of woman in the past as described in the classical texts.

Earlier Status of Woman

In the Vedic age women enjoyed social status equal to that of man. It however started declining during the age of Brahmans (1500-500B.C.) and touched its lowest level with the beginning of the British period. Describing the status of Hindu Woman during the Vedic age, Promila Kapur (1972: 47) writes: "In the Vedic Age (2500-1500B.C.) women had considerable freedom to move about in the family and society and they took an intelligent part in public affairs. They were educated like boys. Marriage used to take place at the age of 16 or 17. They had effective voice in the selection of their partners. Occasional accounts of love marriage are also found. In social and religious gatherings they occupied a prominent position. Women had absolute equality in the eyes of religion. In the family the status of wife and mother was an honoured one. Ordinarily monogamy was the rule. Widow marriage was permitted". Prabhu (1963: 258) and Kapadia (1966:252) state similar opinions about the status of woman during the Vedic Age.

During the age of Brahmans (1500-500B.C.), however, there were "gradual changes in the status of woman" (P. Kapoor; 1972: 47), which further deteriorated during the age of Sutras and Epics (500 B.C. to A.D. 500) (Kurian, 1961 : 16). There was further deterioration in the status of women during the age of Smritis (A.D.); it reached its lowest point during the Muslim rule when women "had almost no status in the society and none in their own estimation" (P. Kapur, 1972: 48). "The invasion of the country by Muslims", according to Kurian (1961:20) "brought about further deterioration in the liberal trend that then existed. On the one hand, the Muslim conquerors attempted to impose their coercive norms on the conquered Hindu population, but, on the other hand, the Hindu society itself became more and more rigid curtailing the rights of woman...."

The position of women touched the lowest ebb during the early British period. Describing the state of affairs during this period, P. Kapur (1976:67) writes: "Child marriage was the general rule for all respectable castes of Hindus, sati was widely prevalent and widows were badly treated. Purdah was strictly enforced among Muslims and to a considerable extent on Hindu women too. Female illiteracy was widespread with negligible exceptions. Polygamy was practised by all those who could afford it. Prostitution was rampant".

The status of woman during this period, i.e., Mughal and early British period which was taken as the norm for assessing the changes if any that had taken place in modern times. The following attributes were taken into account:

i. Birth of a girl was less welcome than that of a boy because a boy was considered to be the rescuer of his father from hell;[1] he alone could offer 'tarpan' to the deceased soul of his father; he perpetuated the 'Kul', added working hands to the family, and fetched dowry, etc.
ii. Since child marriage was the general practice, girls had no schooling or any formal education. They could not sit for University Examinations.[2]
iii. Women had to observe purdah, especially before their elders and outsiders.
iv. Women could not go out of their family occupation to take up independent jobs.

One can legitimately presume that the status of woman has been changing in their favour. This is mostly because of the extensive social reform movements, which started during the later part of the British period, under the leadership of devoted social reformers from Raja Ram Mohan Rai to Maharshi Karve. Their efforts were strengthened by laws enacted by the British Government, which provided women with legal claims and rights. Sati Pratha came to an end; education of girls gained popularity; age-at-marriage increased; seeking employment gained acceptability; and widow remarriage ceased to be a taboo. At present women participate freely in all spheres of social life. Such changes in the life of women in a society may well be supposed to affect the attitudes, thinking, and behaviour of all those men who imposed restrictions on them and also of those women who suffered in silence.

To find out what the position was vis-a-vis the industrial workers, we asked the opinion of the respondents on the various attributes:

Birth of Girls

It has rightly been suggested that "The position of a woman in society can be judged by the way in which the birth of a girl is received" (Shastri, 1960: 2). The respondents were, therefore, asked whether they welcomed or did not welcome, or were indifferent to the birth of a girl. Nearly half of the respondents (48.9%) reported that the birth of a female child was taken by them indifferently: they were neither happy nor unhappy over it; 32.2% reported that the birth of a girl was as auspicious as that of boy, since both were "God's gifts"; 18.9%, however, frankly confessed their unhappiness over the birth of a daughter, because she was a liability as she had to be provided dowry. The reaction of the majority of the respondents towards girls' birth was one of indifference, but they were keen on having a son, because as Prabhu (1963: 242) says, "The son rescues the soul of the deceased ancestors from the hell into which they might fall without his birth."

Education of Girls

Education of girls is considered to be one of the important determinants of a woman's status and has a bearing on the nature and functioning of the joint family system. Kapadia (966:267) observes that "The educated wife is expected to be a companion who will share his [husband's] interests, go with him to clubs and films, sports and parks, and thus be united emotionally with him". This emotional attachment between husband and wife "would tend to destroy the stability of the joint family..." (Gore, 1968 : 7). Kapadia (1966:268) observes that "Education has brought women out of the confines of the house and put them into contact with the philosophy of liberalism and the democratic traditions of the West. It has deferred the age of marriage and enabled women to exercise their choice in the selection of a partner. It has also brought about a new relationship between husband and wife".

Respondents' Education and Attitude Towards the Education of Girls

In the light of these observations, we have in this sub-section studied the respondents' attitude towards girls' education, and have attempted to assess its possible effect on the joint family system. Table 7.1 shows that 96% of them are in favour of girls' education, irrespective of the level of their own education. Only 4% respondents, who are themselves illiterate, are against it. They were of the opinion that education made them less obedient, more fashionable, and unmanageable. They felt that the kind of education that girls need – training in household affairs, such as cooking, stitching, knitting, obedience to elders etc. – was not imparted in modern schools.

Table 7.1 also shows that there is a considerable difference of opinion about the level to which girls can be educated. Respondents having lower education prefer lower level of education for girls, and vice versa. But a note-worthy feature is that respondents of all categories have suggested a level higher than that of their own; 58.3% are in favour of their education upto higher secondary and about 28% upto college level or even higher. As far back as 1955, in a Public Opinion Survey, two-thirds of the total respondents said that it was desirable to give higher education to girls.[3]

TABLE 7.1 **Respondents' Attitude Towards the Education of Girls : by Level of Education**

S. No.	Respondents' Level of Education	Level of Education Preferred						
		Nil	Primary	Middle	Higher Secondary	College	Higher	Total
1.	Nil	16 (23.8)	12 (18.0)	22 (32.8)	10 (15.0)	7 (10.4)	- (-)	67 (100.0)
2.	Primary (1-5)	- (-)	- (-)	5 (12.8)	25 (64.2)	9 (23.0)	- (-)	39 (100.0)
3.	Middle (6-8)	- (-)	- (-)	- (-)	100 (90.0)	11 (10.0)	- (-)	111 (100.0)
4.	Interme-diate (9-12)	- (-)	- (-)	- (-)	95 (56.2)	40 (23.6)	34 (20.2)	169 (100.0)
5.	College	- (-)	- (-)	- (-)	- (-)	- (-)	8 (100.0)	8 (100.0)
	Total	16 (4.0)	12 (3.0)	27 (7.0)	230 (58.3)	67 (17.1)	42 (10.6)	394 (100.0)

Residential Background and Attitude Towards the Education of Girls

The break-up of the respondents' opinion on the education of girls on the basis of their residential background shows that while every native respondent favours education of girls, about 5% of migrant respondents do not. 95% native respondents want the education level to be upto the eighth standard; 83% migrant want the level to be upto higher secondary and above; 8% want it upto the eighth standard, and 4% upto primary. This shows that almost all the respondents, irrespective of their residential background, are in favour of girls' education.

The opinion of respondents on girls' education was tested on the basis of whether they were giving education to their daughters or not. Of the 394 total respondents, 16, who objected to the idea of giving education to girls, were not sending their daughters to school. Of the remaining, 55 had no daughters, and the daughters of 23 respondents were not of school-going age. The remaining 300 had their daughters in schools.

A number of migrant also mentioned that it would not have been possible for them to educate their children had they not brought them to the city. This indicates that with more migration from rural to urban areas, there will be an increase in the number of women who would be educated.

Keeping these factors in view, one can foresee the possible rapid expansion of female education in the future. This would widen the horizons of their knowledge and thinking, broaden their vision, infuse confidence in them, increase their desire and possibilities of self dependence, and help them in the development of their personality and individuality. Coupled with other environmental effects, such developments will drive passiveness out of them and make them vigorous and active. This change in women is expected to make them assertive of their demands for legitimate rights and oppose their oppression and subjugation by other members of the family. Besides, educated girls will be married at a relatively advanced age, when they are emotionally mature. This will lead to a stronger emotional closeness between husband and wife. The superiority of conjugal bond over other filial bonds will presumably weaken the authority of elders. All these hold out a potent threat for the joint family system.

The Purdah System

Purdah system among women is a symbol of their lower status. It segregated them from the mainstream of social life, the elders of the family, and also their own husbands in the presence of their elders. Women were supposed to go inside the house or into their own room, if a stranger or an elder male of the family appeared on the scene. If it was not possible, they were supposed to cover their face. Also, were they not supposed to go outside for work or for any other purpose without covering their face. Purdah also meant confining their movement to the households. They were generally allowed to be in the main portion of the house, and men would live and operate from another portion of the building known as 'Baithak' or 'Dalan'. They would not generally enter the area earmarked for women without informing them through some kind of sound like warning coughs, striking their stick against the ground heavily, or calling some minor child by name. Women would rarely enter the area of men, even in their absence. Purdah was not limited only to hiding one's face or one's own person; it also implied that women were not supposed to talk in the presence of male elders. If it was necessary, they would talk through the medium of some child, or very slowly turning their face away from the adressee.

Whatever might have been the reason for the origin of the purdah system, it left a definite mark on social life: (i) It segregated women from men; women were mostly confined to the four walls of a house; and (ii) women were expected to be deferential towards elders. These two things made women look up to men for everything in their lives, irrespective of what women were like. Further, it bred a feeling in women that they were incomplete in themselves; this made them accept themselves as inferior to men. This was very conducive for the continuation of large households in the joint family system. But lately there have been many changes in this situation. Women have cast off their purdah and have moved away from seclusion. It is probably because of these developments that "The abolition of purdah is frequently reported in accounts of contemporary Hindu life, and today many women do not follow its rules" (Goode, 1963: 250).

We have in this sub-section tried to find out the extent to which the purdah system is being observed by the women of industrial workers, and to know the respondents' opinion on its continuation to find out the impact of the purdah system on the joint family system as well as in predicting its future.

Observance of Purdah System

Our enquiry reveals that purdah system still remains a widely observed practice among the industrial workers. In 73.6% households, women observe purdah in one form or the other and in the remaining households (26.4%), women do not do so (Table 7.2). In the families in which women observe purdah, they do so in different forms and in different measures depending on the people before whom it is to be observed.

TABLE 7.2: **Observance of Purdah in Respondents' Families: by Residential Background**

S. No.	Residential Background	Is Purdah observed in your Family? Yes	No	Total
1.	Native	24	39	63
		(38.0)	(62.0)	(100.0)
2.	Migrant	266	65	331
3.		(80.3)	(19.7)	(100.0)
	Total	290	104	394
		(73.6)	(26.4)	(100.0)

The aggregate percentages reveal that purdah system still remains a common practice. What is significant from our point of view is the distribution of respondents for and against this system in accordance with their residential background. Purdah system is more prevalent among the families of migrant than that of native: about 80% migrants' family observe purdah; the corresponding percentage for native is only 38. Although adequate information regarding the purdah practice in their related families living in the villages could not be obtained, almost all of them reported that women living with them in the city were less conscious of purdah, compared to women in the related families in the village. They said that with women in purdah it was very difficult to manage in the city. With menfolk away at the factory–in day-shift or night-shift–women had to look after the family affairs. This shows that the urban setting has been instrumental in the removal of purdah among migrants.

Besides, the traditional intensity of purdah system seems to have lessened. Compared to the earlier practice of observing purdah before elders and running away from strangers, women of only 27.5% industrial workers' families observe purdah in the presence of strangers; 32.7% families did so in the presence of elder males of the family; and about 40% families did so from both elders and strangers.

The intensity of the system may be said to have decreased also because of changes in the form of purdah observed. As reported by the respondents, majority of women (Table 7.3) turn away their face only from elders and strangers. Only a small minority observed purdah in its traditional form i.e., hiding or keeping away from elders or strangers, or both.

TABLE 7.3: **Forms of Purdah from Elders and Strangers**

S. No.	Forms of Purdah	From whom			Total
		Elders	Strangers	Both	
1.	Hiding away	8 (8.5)	12 (15.1)	6 (5.3)	26 (9.1)
2.	Covering face with 'Goonghat'	22 (23.1)	17 (21.2)	18 (15.6)	57 (19.6)
3.	Turning away face	65 (68.4)	51 (63.7)	91 (79.1)	207 (71.3)
	Total	95 (100.0)	80 (100.0)	115 (100.0)	290 (100.0)

Opinion Regarding Purdah System

Whether purdah system will continue in its present form or will gradually disappear would by and large depend on the attitude of the present generation, both men and women. We have, therefore, also tried to know the respondents' opinion regarding the purdah system, which is presented on the basis of their residential background and level of education in table 7.4. Responses have been tabulated in the form of 'Yes' and 'No' i.e. whether or not they approved of the purdah system.

The table shows that the majority of native respondents (60.3%) did not favour purdah system whereas only about one-third of migrant respondents (33.6%) were against it. This is possibly because of their residential background.

Secondly, there was a positive relationship between the level of education and the disapproval of purdah system, at least in the case of native respondents: as the level of education increases the percentage of those who disfavour purdah system increases from 18% to 100%. Almost a similar pattern can be observed in the case of migrant respondents though not in the same proportion.

TABLE 7.4: **Respondents' Attitude towards Purdah System: by Residential Background and Level of Education**

Sr. No.	Respondents' Educational Level	Residential Native			Background Migrant			Total		
		Yes	No	Total	Yes	No	Total	Yes	No	Total
1.	Nil	9 (81.8)	2 (18.2)	11 (100.0)	50 (89.2)	6 (10.8)	56 (100.00)	59 (88.0)	8 (12.0)	67 (100.00)
2.	1-5 (Primary)	4 (100.00)	- (-)	4 (100.00)	32 (91.4)	3 (8.6)	35 (100.00)	36 (92.3)	3 (7.7)	39 (100.00)
3.	6-8 (Middle)	8 (53.3)	7 (46.7)	15 (100.00)	68 (70.8)	28 (29.2)	96 (100.00)	76 (68.4)	35 (31.6)	111 (100.00)
4.	9-12 (Intermediate)	4 (13.4)	26 (86.6)	30 (100.00)	70 (50.3)	69 (49.7)	139 (100.00)	74 (43.8)	95 (56.2)	169 (100.00)
5.	College	- (-)	3 (100.00)	3 (100.00)	- (-)	5 (100.00)	5 (100.00)	- (-)	8 (100.00)	8 (100.00)
	Total	25 (39.7)	38 (60.3)	63 (100.00)	220 (66.4)	111 (33.6)	331 (100.00)	245 (62.1)	149 (37.9)	394 (100.00)

Finally, considering the second inference and the expansion of education, purdah system is likely to lose favour even among the workers who have migrated from villages to the city.

Opinions regarding the continuance of purdah system have been tabulated age-wise in table 7.5. It shows that the percentage of respondents who favour the system increase with increase in the age-groups of the respondents: 64% respondents belonging to the age-group of 18-35 years favoured purdah system, the percentage for the two following age-groups increased to 78.8% and 84% respectively. Similarly, the percentage of respondents against purdah system decreased from 36% for the age-group of 18-35 years to 16% for the oldest age group (45-60 years). Although the percentage of respondents belonging to younger generation favouring purdah system was as high as 64%, the trend did indicate a gradual slackening in the purdah system when a comparison of corresponding percentages related to other age-groups was made. It may, therefore, be expected that purdah will be observed by a smaller number of women in future.

TABLE 7.5: **Respondents' Attitude Towards Purdah System: by Age-groups**

S.No	Respondents' Age Groups	Do you favour Purdah System Yes		No		Total
		No. of Resps.	% *	No. of Resps.	% *	
	1	2	3	4	5	6
1.	(18-35)	123	64.0	66	36.0	189
2.	(36-45)	89	78.8	24	21.2	113
3.	(46-60)	78	84.0	14	16.0	92
	Total	290	73.6	104	26.4	394

* percentages refer to the total number of respondents in each age-group (col. 6)

To sum up, our study of purdah system reveals that this system is likely to disappear gradually leading to the rise in the status of women within the family and in the larger social framework. Such a rise will have an adverse impact on the joint family system.

Employment of Women Outside the Family

It was "uncommon for a woman in the traditional Hindu family to accept employment outside home" (Gore, 1968: 159), because "It was considered derogatory for a woman to take work outside the home" (Kapadia, 1966: 263). The customary prohibition on women's employment outside the family would naturally make them dependent for their needs on the earnings of the male members of the family, and lower their status in comparison to men. But economic compulsions, rising standards of living, availability of jobs, increasing number of educated women, governmental encouragement to women in recruitment policy, and the impact of western ideology has changed the attitude of people towards the employment of women.

In view of this, we tried to know the attitude of our respondents towards the employment of women. To make our enquiry more specific, the respondents were asked whether they liked women, in general, accepting employment outside the family and whether they would like to send their wives to accept jobs outside their homes. The responses obtained in reply to the enquiry are presented in table 7.6.

TABLE 7.6: **Attitude Towards Employment of Women: by Respondents' Age**

S.No.	Age-Group	Yes	No	Total
1.	18-35	166 (87.8)	23 (12.2)	189 (100.00)
2.	36-45	61 (53.9)	52 (46.1)	113 (100.00)
3.	46-60	5 (5.5)	87 (94.5)	92 (100.00)
	Total	232 (58.8)	162 (41.2)	394 (100.00)

The figures presented in the table 7.6 show that the majority of the respondents (58.8%) favoured the idea of women going for paid employment outside the family. About 41% respondents were against it for two reasons: (i) it indicated a fall in social prestige in the 'Biradari', and (ii) led to dislocation and mismanagement in household affairs. The responses show that some oppose the idea mainly because of their traditional outlook, and others do so on rational grounds. The differing attitudes of the respondents seem to have a close association with their age. If we compare the percentages of respondents in different age-groups favouring outdoor employment, we find that the younger generation of workers favour the idea in much greater measure than the workers of older generation: 87.8% workers of the age-group 18-35 considered the idea desirable. This fell to 53.9% in case of the respondents of age-group 36-45 and to 5.5% in 46-60 years age-group.

In addition to the study of general attitude of the workers towards the employment of women outside the family, we also tried to know whether respondents would allow their wives to go out for jobs. Their responses showed that percentage of those who would actually allow their wives to take up outdoor jobs is 46.9%, which is less than the people who considered it desirable to allow women to take jobs (58.8%). Those who would not like their wives to take jobs account for 51.7%. The majority of those who would not like their wives working out does so for domestic reasons while the minority does so on account of loss in social prestige. This, however, does not materially alter the conclusion that majority is in favour of women's employment.

Unlike the variables already mentioned, there does not seem to be much variation in the attitude of respondents towards women's employment on the basis of their residential background. While 66.6% native respondents were in favour of this, the corresponding percentage for migrant respondents was 57.4%. These two percentages together account for 58.8% of the respondents favouring women going out to take jobs. Observing the same changes in the attitudes of people towards employment of women, Kapadia (1959:99) says: "Today even the members of the older generation desire that the educated daughter-in-law must help the family by supplementing its income".

Our overall assessment of the attitude of the respondents towards employment of women outside their household is that a majority is not against it. Although wives of only 4 workers are working outside their home, others who expressed their willingness to allow their wives to go out for job would expectedly do so if suitable[4] jobs were available–and as the trend shows that they will–the number of working women even of the industrial workers will increase. If it happens, she will certainly add to the family income and "A working woman who makes a more or less significant contribution to the family income also feels that she should have a share in decision making process" (Ramanujam, 1972: 28). Kapadia (1966: 263) also observes that a "... woman can now be economically strong and assertive". After the woman starts earning and becomes an economic asset to the family, she will naturally like to assert her position. With her changing position she may not readily accept the subordinate position assigned to her in the traditional family, which may ultimately weaken the joint family system.

NOTES

1. Kapadid (1966: 258): "We find in the literature of this period—Manusamhita as well as the Mahabharata—a derivation of the word *Putra*, son as one who saves the father from going to hell (*Put*)."
2. Kapadia (1966: 167): "...when in the year 1875 one Khursteji Postmaster asked the Syndicate of Bombay University to permit his daughter to appear for the Matriculation examination, the Syndicate refused permission because they thought that the University Act did not allow it."
3. Monthly Public Opinion Surveys of the Indian Institute of Public Opinion. 1 (Nov. 1955: 38).
4. Almost all the workers willing to send their wives out for jobs invariably mentioned this term.

EIGHT

Summary And Conclusions

The Problem

There has been a good deal of controversy over the present state of the institution of joint family. Some sociologists are of the opinion that this institution is as strong today as it ever was. Some others feel that it is disintegrating. A perusal of the existing scholarship shows that this diversity of opinions has its origin in the varied definitions adopted by sociologists. Besides, their attempt to generalise their findings on the basis of a study of a small sample of some section of our society has also added to this controversy.

To have a clearer perspective of the problem, many prominent sociologists have suggested that the institution be studied by accommodating it to the changing socio-economic conditions. In this re-appraisal, the emphasis has shifted from the traditional to the non-traditional concept of the joint family: from the traditional characteristics of such a family, common kitchen, common property, and common deity etc. to the non-traditional concept which lays emphasis on the functional relationships between affinal households and inter-personal relationships thereof and not on household dimensions only.

Some studies, such as those of Desai and Singer, have already been undertaken on these lines for different sections of our society. But many other sections of the society have yet to be studied, and prominent among them is the class of industrial workers. Existing studies on them do not say much on their family systems; besides, they are not based on the non-traditional approach (interationist approach). So there still remains much scope for the study of the family system of industrial workers.

Under the changing socio-economic conditions, the study of the family system of industrial workers on the basis of a non-traditional approach can prove helpful in knowing the present state of the institution. It was in view of this that the present study was undertaken. It deals with the family system of a sample of industrial workers working in a prominent textile Mill of a metropolitan town–Delhi. The basic reason that prompted us to select this particular section of our society was its migratory character–its movement from the native place, usually a village, to the city where the Mill is located. Migration inevitably leads to the settlement of a 'branch family' in an urban atmosphere, away from the root family, It causes 'structural nucleation' or at least a bifurcation of the family. The structural bifurcation may be supposed to weaken the family bonds between the units (due to distancing in time and space) and may ultimately lead to a complete nucleation of the families. Such a situation provides an ideal social milieu for studying the institution of the joint family.

The Sample

For the purpose of this study a sample of 7% was drawn from the list of permanent workers of Delhi Cloth Mills, Delhi with Department as strata [1]. The sample yielded 394 workers.

Purpose of Study

The main purpose of this study was to study the present pattern of the joint family system among industrial workers, especially from the functional point of view as also to attempt a possible statement on the future of this institution in a specific industrial context. Since the traditional mode of looking at the jointness of a family was found inadequate for getting the right feel of what the situation was now, it was found feasible to look at the concept of jointness in a family from a functional point of view. What follows is a summary of the major conclusions of our investigation. Since assessing the future of the joint family also formed a part of the investigation, a separate section discusses some of our findings in this regard.

In pursuance of our objectives, we addressed ourselves to the following questions:

i. Whether 'structural nucleation' of the families caused by migration or any other factor leads to 'functional nucleation' as well or allows this unit to function as an extension of the joint family from which it has come. In other words, whether respondents' nuclear unit is only a nuclear household maintaining functional relations with other affinal households or whether it has become completely a nuclear family as well by breaking away from, and snapping all its functional relations with, the households of their parents and/or brothers.

ii. whether compositionally or structurally joint families are joint functionally as well, and

iii. whether the existing pattern coincides with the traditional pattern.

In our attempt to find answers to these questions we commenced our study with certain hypotheses. The major ones may be briefly stated as below: [2]

i. Industrial occupation calls for physical mobility from rural to urban areas, and, therefore, the structure of family tilts towards nuclearity.

ii. Establishment of nuclear units reduces the degree of contact, weakens relationship with other kinship group(s) and thereby reduces the degree of jointness of the family in the form of fulfillment of mutual obligations, etc.

Although the main focus of our study is on migrant industrial workers, we have also included native industrial workers in our study to draw comparisons and to have a more comprehensive view of the family system. Besides, the inclusion of their pattern of family system would also help as an indicator of the likely pattern of the family system of the migrant workers.

The Approach

In our study we have considered both the traditional and non-traditional concepts of the joint family system. In our approach to the problem, we have first of all studied household structure of the industrial workers (both migrant and native) mainly on the basis of their kinship composition and generation depth. We found that 62.5% of migrant and 8.9% of native households are nuclear and 21.3% of migrant and 7.3% native workers are living in joint households. These households were then studied along the following lines:

i. Functional relationships between respondents' nuclear households and the households of their parents and/or brothers;
ii. functional relationships between the various nuclear units constituting the joint households; and
iii. inter-personal relationships between the members of both nuclear and joint households.

After studying the households on the basis of functional jointness, we have tried to find out nuclearity of nuclear households and jointness of joint households, the traditionally joint families.

Finally, on the basis of differences in the responses of the respondents of different residential backgrounds, different age groups, different levels of educations, and the respondents' attitude towards and their opinions on the institution of marriage and status of women, we have tried to indicate the likely changes expected in the institution of the joint family.

Findings

The Structural Aspect

It is commonly believed that given its kinship composition, the traditional form of family in India, especially among the Hindus, was that of a joint family; it was a real living actuality.[3] Contrary to this our findings (Chapter III) revealed that nearly three-fourths (71.4%) of the households were nuclear which according to the traditional norms, can be considered as nuclear families. Only the remaining (28.6%) households have the features of joint families. The preponderance of nuclear households exists despite the fact that all the sample workers have parents, and/or major earning brothers, and/or sons. And, if they wanted to live together or if circumstances had permitted, they could have lived in lineally or fraternally joint households. It is noteworthy that the nuclear households in the case of our respondents have come into existence essentially as a result of bifurcation between the respondents' and their parents and/or brothers or sons. This supports our hypothesis that working in an industrial concern calls for physical mobility from rural to urban areas, and, therefore, the structure of family tilts towards nuclearity.

However, splitting of families into different units is not a new phenomenon.[4] Even in old days when the family size would grow unmanageable a split was an inevitable concomitant. But the modern phenomenon of nuclearity of industrial workers is not based on unmanageability of the household size, but on a number of other factors, such as the search for new ways and means of livelihood. A new dimension of this phenomenon is the nucleation of families due to clashes and conflicts between members of a family. For instance, our findings reveal that out of the total splits between parents and sons 26(19.1%) and between brothers 106 (72.5%) took place due to clashes, particularly between womenfolk, and on issues like undue interference of the elders, and unwillingness of the younger generation to share the responsibilities of the joint households.

The trend of nucleation due to splits caused by clashes on different issues are more prominent among native than among migrant: as many as 86% nuclear households among the native were formed as a result of clashes, while among the migrant the percentage of nuclear households formed due to clashes was only 42%.

The Functional Aspect

After examining the structure of families, we attempted to find out whether a structurally nuclear family can be regarded also as a functionally nuclear family or not. The same question arises with respect to joint households adjudged as joint families on the basis of their characteristics of a traditional joint family.

In our attempt to answer these questions we have studied both nuclear and joint households on the basis of criteria of functional jointness in the family (Chapter IV).

To assess the extent of jointness between the respondents' nuclear households and the households of their parents and/or brothers we employed the following criteria: (i) feeling and fulfillment of financial obligations, (ii) reciprocal visits, (iii) seeking advice and approval of elders, and (iv) rendering/exchange of personal services. On the basis of these criteria[5] nuclear households were categorised into (i) Closely related, (ii) Marginally related, and (iii) Nuclear. Households falling in the first two categories were considered as functionally joint families and marginally joint families correspondingly, in spite of their 'structural nuclearity' and residential separation. Only the households falling in the third category were designated as Nuclear families because they fulfillèd neither the structural nor the functional criteria of jointness.

On the basis of feeling and fulfillment of financial obligations, as many as 87.1% nuclear households were found closely related, 7.4% marginally related to their parental households, and only 5.5% were nuclear. The corresponding percentages in the case of fraternal households were 30.9, 26.0, and 43.1, respectively (Table 4.18). Clearly, closeness towards parents exists in a much larger measure than towards brothers. Further, compared on the basis of residential background, a higher proportion of migrant was closely related to both parents and brothers than their native counterparts. (Table 4.7).

On the basis of our second criterion--paying reciprocal visits--we found 67.8% nuclear households to be closely and 23.7% marginally related to parental households; 8.5% are nuclear. The corresponding percentages for the fraternal households are 64.3, 15.7 and 20.0 respectively (Table 4.18). These figures also indicate that lineal links, by and large, are stronger than the fraternal ones. Here, too there is a substantial difference between native and migrant respondents: migrant are closer to parental as well as fraternal households than their native counterparts (Table 4.14). It is noteworthy that migrant respondents, in spite of living farther off from their parental and fraternal households, were found to be closer to their affinal households in comparison to their native counterparts whose parents and brothers are living in the same city. The study, therefore, shows that spatial separation and distance do not radically affect the frequency of visits and the expression of concern about one's relations. Our findings thus negate a part of the hypothesis that "establishment of nuclear families away from the parental residence decreases the frequency of contacts".

On the basis of the third criterion--seeking advice and approval of elders--42% were found to be closely related and 52.4% marginally related to parental households; the remaining 5.6% were nuclear. The coresponding percentages for fraternal households are 18.9, 28.3, and 52.8% respectively (Table 4.18). This reinforces our findings about the existence of a higher degree of lineal jointness. A comparison between native and migrant respondents also shows native to be less close to their affinal households than their migrant counterparts: about 41% of native households do not consult their elders or seek their advice or approval, whereas the corresponding percentage for their migrant counterpart is only 13 (Table 4.15).

Significantly enough, the percentages of closely related households is lowest on the basis of this criterion. It indicates that dependence on the advice and approval of elders is showing a declining trend. It may be understandable in the case of migrant because of the distance factor, but this trend in the case of native does reveal the gradual disappearance of the prerogative of the elders to advise the young ones.

So far as rendering/exchanging of mutual services, our fourth criterion, is concerned, it was found to be very much prevalent: as many as 97.5% respondents were found closely related to their parents and 76.0% to their brothers (Table 4.18). Here too one finds a difference between lineal and fraternal jointness. No significant difference was observed between native and migrant respondents in this regard.

If we combine our findings in regard to jointness of the respondents' nuclear households and the households of their parents and brothers on the basis of the four criteria, two different patterns emerge: (I) in relation to parents, and (II) in relation to brothers.

(I) Jointness continues to exist to a large extent between parents and sons on almost all criteria of functional jointness. Sons rendering personal services to their parents have by and large a feeling for them and are fulfilling financial obligations towards them, and are paying frequent visits to them, though it is at the lowest level and markedly away from the traditional pattern so far as "seeking advice and approval of elders" is concerned. There are no doubt deviants in respect of all the functional criteria of jointness but their number is too small. There is, however, a definite evidence to indicate that over-all jointness is more prevalent among migrant than in the case of native. Further, compared on the basis of age, it is more prevalent among the older people than among the younger ones.

(II) Compared with lineal jointness, fraternal jointness is difinitely on the decline , though it still exists to a reasonably good extent so far as rendering/exchanging of personal services and reciprocal visits is concerned. But in regard to feeling and fulfillment of financial obligations, the relatively more important test of jointness, our findings reveal that very few people are ready to help their brothers financially, and support our hypothesis that "An individual earner in an urban area seems to have a tendency not to share his fortune with other affinal relations. Therefore, the degree of jointness in the form of fulfillment of mutual obligations is affected adversely by the establishment of a separate nuclear family..."

The relatively lower degree of jointness between fraternal groups is also supported by a declining trend in the authority of elder brothers compared to that of parents: only 18.9% reported to be closely related to their fraternal households against 42.0% to parents. Further, lineal and fraternal jointness are stronger amongst migrant than among native.

Looking at age as a variable, the respondents of older age group are more closely related even to their fraternal households than to their counterparts in the younger age group.

Joint Households

So far as joint households are concerned they are all structurally or compositionally joint. They can be designated as joint families as well when assessed on the basis of the traditional characteristics of a joint family. But their assessment on the basis of functional criteria shows that only about 70% of them are functionally joint families (Table 4.17(C)). In spite of joint residence, nearly one-third (30.4%) of them are not joint families. Jointness in them is more apparent than real. Further, as in the case of nuclear households, jointness existed to a greater extent in the lineally joint households than in the fraternal ones. Again, like nuclear households, joint households of the migrant respondents are functionally joint families in larger proportion as compared to their native counterparts.

In an over-all comparison of jointness between both nuclear and joint households, we find that lineal jointness exists in a larger proportion than fraternal jointness. On the basis of almost all the criteria of functional jointness, our findings with regard to both structural as well as functional aspects support our hypothesis that "the joint family pattern is expected to be prevalent less in fraternal than in lineal relatives".

Our over-all findings lead us to the conclusion that majority of the joint households are joint families as well when tested on the basis of functional criteria. Nuclear households are not devoid of jointness either. Despite their structural nuclearity, majority of them are functionally joint with their affinal households. Jointness is, however, more prevalent in lineal than in fraternal groups, more in migrant than in native, and more in the older generation than in the younger ones. Also, in spite of a very high degree of jointness among the respondents of nuclear households, a few of them are completely atomised and isolated, and are not at all fused with affinal households. They are not nuclear households, but completely nuclear families. But their number is too small to permit any meaningful generalisation. At the same time, however, our findings do not support the idea of the non-existence of completely nuclear families.

The Inter-personal Relationships

Our findings regarding inter-personal relationships between different sets of relatives are quite revealing. A comparison of our findings with the traditional pattern (Chapter V) brings out the deviations that are evident in inter-personal relations. Neither the father over his son, nor husband over his wife, nor elder brother over his younger brother, nor even mother-in-law over her daughter-in-law enjoys the traditional authority. Another noteworthy feature of our findings is that the authority pattern even in the joint households which have been designated as joint families on the basis of some concrete characteristics of joint family is dwindling. Quite in consonance with our earlier conclusion, we find that with regard to inter-personal relations there is a difference between the behaviour patterns of the migrant and the native: the migrant are more attached to traditional norms than the native. Similarly, the authority pattern between brothers is much weaker than between father and son. If the authority pattern in its tr ditional form had any role to play in the sustenance of the joint f mily the dwindling authority of elders presumanly may affect the insutution in times to come.

The Future Trends

This does not give sufficient evidence to say anything on the possible future trends. But when we look at our sample on the basis of age-composition and the percentages of native and migrant, we can say that forces inimical to the continuance of joint families are on the increase. Young people do not feel themselves attached to the traditional norms of a joint family in the same measure as the older ones do. Further, jointness exists because of the heavy percentage of migrants who are for joint families. If, with the passage of time, migrants gradually take to the ways of native--which is a logical assumption--it can be said that jointness that our sample brings out may not continue for long.

However, to be on a sound ground in indicating the future of joint families, we elicited opinions of our respondents on two powerful cementing forces in the traditional joint family, i.e., the institution of marriage and the status of woman. The different aspects of the institution of marriage we have considered are: (i) age-at-marriage, (ii) process of mate-selection, and (iii) widow remarriage. The prevalence of these aspects in a particular form and the role they played in the sustenance of joint family have been established beyond doubt (Chapter VI). The respondents in an overwhelming majority--particularly the younger, educated, and the native--were against the continuity of such practices as child marriage, giving little or no freedom of mate-selection to the concerned parties and prohibition of widow marriage. If the trend continues to be the same and the people of coming generation insist on the marriage of their children at a comparatively older age, give them freedom in mate-selection, and encourage widow marriage, the institution of joint family would possibly weaken, at least to the extent it was maintained by these customs. We find that the traditional pattern of age-at-marriage and process of mate-selection was followed vigorously by the respondents of the older generation than by the younger one. We also find that the older the respondent the lower the age at his marriage, and vice versa. Incidentally, none of the respondents of the older age-group (46-60) was consulted in the selection of his spouse; only 10.7% amongst the middle age-group were consulted and the percentage rose to 18.9 in the case of respondents of the youngest age-group. The younger respondents expressed more liberal opinions on these practices. This indicates a likelihood of increase in the age-at-marriage. This, coupled with freedom in mate-selection, would bring husband and wife closer and lead to the strengthening of conjugal ties making the consanguineal ties subordinate to the former. This may work as a powerful, potential threat to the continuity of the institution of joint family. Changing attitudes towards widow marriage may also play their role; 58.8% favour it. What is more important in this regard is that it is not being considered a taboo even by the older people. Deviations from the traditional norm are widespread in this area too.

In the old pattern the lower status of women in and outside the family vis-a-vis their male counterparts was said to be of immense help in the sustenance of the joint family (Chapter VII). This was possible by observing certain prescribed behaviour patterns which do not find favour now. Our respondents are generally in favour of female education, and the employment of women outside their households, and are against the observance of purdah system in its traditional form. The younger, native, and the educated were much critical of the past practices in this regard. Changes in all these attributes are expected to elevate woman's status in the family as well as in her social life. She may not then be prepared to lead a life of subjugation in the family and this might endanger the stability of the joint family system. All these changes would positively affect the structural form of the family and in turn the functional aspect of the institution of the joint family.

It is difficult to draw conclusions on the basis of a limited sample. Despite our limitations the following conclusions seem permissible:

(i) There is a preponderance of nuclear households or structurally nuclear families.

(ii) In spite of residential separation feeling of jointness towards parents exists in a large measure in the form of rendering of personal services and feeling for and fulfillment of financial obligations.

(iii) Jointness towards brothers, though in existence, is very weak when compared with that of parents.

(iv) Jointness towards parents as well as brothers is weaker among the urban than among the rural.

(v) Joint households or structurally joint families are not necessarily joint families functionally.

(vi) Authority pattern is weaker as compared to the normative pattern. It is however, weaker in fraternal than in lineal groups. Also, compared on the basis of residential background, it is weaker among the urban than among the rural.

(vii) A comparison on the basis of age as a variable and opinions of respondents on certain cementing forces of joint family does not show a bright future for the institution of the joint family.

NOTES

1. Detailed characteristics of Sample workers are given in Chapter II.
2. Hypotheses have been given in detail in Chapter I.
3. Dhirendra Narain (1970:454): "Joint family was not a normative pattern but was an actual arrangement".
4. Desai (1964: 31) "Infinite jointness of a given group would mean the whole society eventually becoming one joint family which is an absurdity."
5. Details in Chapter IV.

Select Bibliography

Abbi, B.L. "Urban Family in India", *Contributions to Indian Sociology*, New Series, (1969) No. 3, pp. 116-127

Acharya, Hemalatha. "Some Possible Variations in Family Types in Gujarat", in George Kurian (ed.), *The Family in India - A Regional View* (The Hague: Mouton Paris, 1974), pp. 179-90.

Agarwala, B.R. "In a Mobile Commercial Community", in "Symposium on Caste and Joint Family", *Sociological Bulletin*, vol. 4, no. 2 (1955), pp. 138-45.

Aiyappan, A. "In Tamilnad" in "Symposium on Caste and Joint Family", *Sociological Bulletin*, vol. 4, no. 2 (1955), pp. 117-22.

Audinarayana, N. "Age at Marriage and its determinants among the Hindus and the Muslims in Rural Andhra Pradesh". Doctoral dissertation, (Sri Venkateswara University, 1985)

Bailey, F.G. "The Joint Family in India: A Framework for Discussion", *The Economic Weekly*, XII (1960), pp. 345-52.

Baruah, Geetanjali. *"Family structure among some tea garden labourers of Assam"*, Bull Cult Res Inst. 14 (1-2), 1980, pp. 73-79.

Bhadra, R.K. "Some observations on family research in India" *Indian Journal of Social Research*. 22(1) April '81, pp. 58-75.

Bhitsten, D.R. *The World of Family* (New York: Random House, 1963).

Bott, Elizabeth. *Family and Social Network* (London: Tavistock Publications, 1957).

Bell, N.W. and Vogel, E.F. (eds.) *A Modern Introduction to the Family* (London: Routledge and Kegan Paul, 1960).

Chakraborty, K. "A note on family research in India". *Socialist Perspective*, 10 (3) Dec. '82. pp. 155-68

Chakraborty, P. and Bhowmick, Samita. "Some aspects of household organisation and family structure in Calcutta". *Eastern Anthropologist*, 36 (1) Jan.Mr. '83 pp. 31-44

Chekki, D.A. "Modernisation and Social Change: The Family and Kin Network in Urban India", in George Kurian (ed.), *The Family in India - A Regional View* (The Hague: Mouton Paris, 1974), pp. 317-34.

Chitnis, Suma. "From Tradition to Modernity: The Family in Transition" in *Femina*, vol. 18, no. 15, A Times of India Publication, July 29 (1977), pp. 18-19.

Cohn, Bernard S. "Chamar Family in a North Indian Village: A Structural Contingent", *The Economic Weekly*, XIII (1961), pp. 1051-55.

Conklin, George H. "The Family Formation Process in India: An Overview", *Journal of Family Welfare*, XIV (1968), pp. 28-37.

-----. "Social Change and the Joint Family: the Causes of Research Biases", *Economic and Political Weekly*, IV (1969), pp. 1445-48.

-----. "Family Structure Caste and Economic Development: An Urban-Rural Comparison from Dharwar", in G.R. Gupta (ed.), *Family and Social Change in Modern India* (New Delhi: Vikas Publishing House Pvt. Ltd., 1976), pp. 19-36

Das, F.H. *Purdah: The Status of Indian Women* (London, 1932).

Das, M.S. and Bardis D.D. "*The Family in Asia*". (New Delhi: Vikas Publishing House, 1978)

Desai, A.R. *Rural Sociology in India* (Bombay: The Indian Society of Agricultural Economics, 1961).

Desai, I.P. *High School Students in Poona* (Poona: Deccan College, 1953).

-----. "Caste and Family", *The Economic Weekly*, VI (1954), pp. 249-54.

-----. "An Analysis" in "Symposium on Caste and Joint Family", *Sociological Bulletin*, IV (1955), pp. 97-117.

-----. "The Joint Family in India -- An Analysis", *Sociological Bulletin*, vol. V, no. 2 (September 1956), pp. 144-56.

-----. *Some Aspects of Family in Mahuwa* (Bombay: Asia Publishing House, 1964).

Driver, Edwin D. "Family Structure and Socio-Economic Status in Central India", *Sociological Bulletin*, XI: 1&2 (March and September 1962), pp. 112-20.

D'Souza, Anthony A. "Introduction" in *The Indian Family in the Change and Challenge of the Seventies* (I.S.I. Publication, New Delhi: Sterling Publishers, 1972), pp. 1-19.

D'Souza, Victor S. "Family Types and Industrialization in India", in George Kurian (ed.), *The Family in India - A Regional View* (The Hague: Mounton, Paris 1974), pp. 151-62.

Dube, S.C. *Indian Village* (London: Routledge & Kegan Paul, 1965).

Dumount, Louis. "Marriage in India: the present State of the Question", *Contributions to Indian Sociology*, V (1961), pp. 75-95.

Ehrenfels, Von V.R. "Matrilineal Joint Family Patterns in India", in George Kurian (ed.), *The Family in India - A Regional View* (The Hague: Mouton, Paris, 1974).

Gandhi, R.S. "A critique for family researches in India", Indian Journal of Social Research, 24 (1) Ap. '83 pp. 41-45.

Ghosh, B.R. "Changes in the Size and Composition of Household Brought about by Urbanization in Delhi Area", in George Kurian (ed.), *The Family in India - A Regional View* (The Hague: Mouton Paris, 1974), pp. 249-62.

Ghurye, G.S. "Social Change in Maharashtra", Part II *Sociological Bulletin*, 3 (March, 1954), pp. 42-50.

Goode, William J. *World Revolution and Family Patterns* (New York: Free Press, 1963).

Gore, M.S. *Urbanization and Family Change* (Bombay: Popular Prakashan, 1968).

Gould, Harold A. "Time Dimension and Structural Change in Indian Kinship System: A Problem of Conceptual Refinement", in Milton Singer and Bernard S. Cohn (eds.), *Structure and Change in Indian Society* (New York: Wenner-Gren Foundation for Anthropological Research, 1968), pp. 413-21.

Gupta, G.R. (ed.). *Family and Social Change in Modern India* (New Delhi: Vikas Publishing House Pvt. Ltd., 1976). pp. xxiii-xxxiv.

Hallen, G.C. (ed.) *Family Researches in India:* Some strategies (Rohini Publications, Shastri Nagar, Meerut).

Hate, C.A. *Changing Status of Woman in Post-Independence India* (Bombay: Allied Publishers, 1969).

Ishwaran, K. "The Interdependence of Elementary and Extended Family", in George Kurian (ed.), *The Family in India - A Regional View* (The Hague: Mouton Paris, 1974), pp. 163-78.

Jejeebhoy, S.J. "Household type and family size in Maharashtra", *Journal of Family Welfare*, 40 (1) Se. '83, pp. 8-22

Jolly. *Encyclopaedia of Religion and Ethics*, Vol. V (ed.) James Hastings (New York, 1960), p. 737.

Kapadia, K.M. "Changing Patterns of Hindu Marriage and Family - I", *Sociological Bulletin*, III (1954a), pp. 61-87.

-----. "Changing Patterns of Hindu Marriage and Family - II", *Sociological Bulletin*, III (1954b), pp. 131-57.

-----. "Changing Patterns of Hindu Marriage and Family - III", *Sociological Bulletin*, IV (1955a), pp. 1961-62.

-----. "Rural Family Patterns: A Study in Urban-Rural Relations", *Sociological Bulletin*, vol. 5, no. 2 (September 1956), pp. 111-26.

-----. *Marriage and Family in India* (Bombay: Oxford University Press, 1966).

Kapoor, Saroj. "Family and Kinship Groups among the Khatris in Delhi", *Sociological Bulletin*, XIV (1965), pp. 54-63.

Kapur, Promilla. "The Changing Role and Status of Women", in *The Indian Family in the Change and Challenge of the Seventies* (I.S.I. Publications, New Delhi: Sterling Publishers (P) Ltd. 1972), pp. 46-59.

-----. "Studies of the Urban Women in India", in G.R. Gupta (ed.), *Family and Social Change in Modern India* (New Delhi: Vikas Publishing House, 1976), pp. 65-102.

Karve, Irawati. *Kinship Organization in India* (Bombay: Asia Publishing House, 1965).

Kay, F.G. *The Family in Transition: Its Past, Present and Future Patterns* (Newton Abbot Devon: David and Charles, 1972).

Kolenda, Pauline M. "Region. Caste and Family Structure: A Comparative Study of the Indian 'Joint' Family", in Milton Singer and Bernard Cohn (eds.), *Structure and Change in Indian Society* (New York: Wenner-Gren Foundation for Anthropological Research, 1968), pp. 339-96.

Kulkarni, M.G. "Family Patterns in Gokak Taluka", *Sociological Bulletin*, IX(1960), pp. 60-81.

Kumar, Joginder. "Family Structure in the Hindu Society of Rural India", in George Kurian (ed.), *The Family in India - A Regional View* (The Hague: Mouton, Paris, 1974), pp. 335-50.

Kurian, George. *Indian Family in Transition:* A Case Study of Kerala Syrian Christians (Mounton & Co. - 'S-Gravenhage, 1961).

-----. "The Indian Family in Transition: Some Regional Variations", in G.R. Gupta (ed.), *Family and Social Change in Modern India* (New Delhi: Vikas Publishing House, 1976), pp. 3-18.

-----. "Child Marriage - A Case Study in Kerala" in Dhirendra Narain (ed.), *Explorations in the Family and Other Essays* (Bombay: Thacker & Co., Ltd., 1975),pp. 206-17.

Lambert, Richard D. *Workers, Factories,. and Social Change in India* (Princeton: Princeton University Press, 1963).

Linton, Ralph. "Cultural and Personality Factors Affecting Growth', in Bert F. Hoselitz (ed.), *The Progress of Underdeveloped Areas* (Chicago: University of Chicago Press, 1952).

Madan, T.N. "The Hindu Joint Family", *Man,* LXII (1962a), pp. 88-89.

-----. "The Joint Family: a Terminological Clarification", *International Journal of Comparative Sociology*, III (1962b), pp. 7-16.

-----. *Family and Kiship*: A Study of the Pandits of Rural Kashmir (Bombay: Asia Publishing House, 1965).

Majumdar, P.S. and Majumdar Ila. *"Rural Migrants in Urban Setting"* (New Delhi: Hindustan Publishing Corporation, 1978)

Mandelbaum, D.G. "The Family in India", in Ruth Nanda Anshen (ed.), *The Family: Its Functions and Destiny* (New York: Harper and Brothers, 1948), p. 93.

-----. *Society in India* (Bombay: Popular Prakashan, 1972).

Matejko, A.J. *The Social Dimensions of Industrialism* (Meerut: Sadhna Prakashan, 1974).

Mehta, Nandini. "The Joint Family: who wants it?" *The Hindustan Times* (Mag.) 1:1-2, 19th Oct. '80.

Merchant, K.T. *Changing Views on Marriage and the Family*: Hindu Youth (Madras: B.G. Paul & Co., 1935).

Merton, Robert K. *Social Theory and Social Structure* (Glencoe: Free Press, 1957).

Mirelle, Abcille. *Indra, the Status of Women in Ancient India* (Banaras: Motilal Banarasidas, 1955).

Morrison, William A. "Family Patterns in Badlapur: An Analysis of a Changing Institution in a Maharashtrian Village", *Sociological Bulletin*, VIII (1959), pp. 45-67.

Mukherjee, Ram Krishna. "On the Classification of Family Structure" in T.N. Madan and Gopala Sarana (eds), *Indian Anthropology: Essays in Memory of D.N. Majumdar* (Bombay: Asia Publishing House, 1962), pp. 352-98.

-----. "Indian Tradition and Social Change" in T.K.N. Unnithan (et. al., eds.,), *Towards a Sociology of Culture in India* (New Delhi: Prentice Hall of India (Private) Ltd., 1965). pp. 189-211.

Narain, Dhirendra. "Interpersonal Relationships in the Hindu Family" in Reuben Hill and Rene Konig (eds.), *Families in East and West* (Paris: The Hague, 1970), pp. 454-80.

Nicholas, Ralph W. "Economics of Family Types in Two West Bengal Villages", *The Economic Weekly*, XIII (1961), pp. 1057-60.

Nimkoff, N.F. and Gore, M.S. "Social Bases of the Hindu Joint Family", *Sociology and Social Research*, XLIV (1959), pp. 27-36.

Nye, F.I. and Berardo, F.M. *The Family - Its Structure and Interaction* (London: Collier Macmillan Publishers, 1973).

O'Malley, L.S.S. *India's Social Heritage* (New Delhi: Vikas Publishing House Pvt. Ltd., 1976).

Orenstein, Henry. "The Recent History of the Extended Family in India", *Social Problems*, VIII (1961), pp. 341-50.

Pakrasi, Kanti. "A Study of Some Aspects of Household Types and Family Organization in Rural Bengal, 1946-1947", *The Eastern Anthropologist*, XV (1962), pp. 55-63.

Parmar S.B.S. "Jointness and nuclearity of the Hindu family in rural setting." *Eastern Anthropologist*, 32(3) J1-Se '79. pp. 193-99

Patel Haribhai, G. "Attitude of urban student youth to age at marriage and family size". *Journal of Family Welfare*, 28 (3) Mar. '82, pp. 58-62

Prabhu, P.H. *Hindu Social Organisation* (Bombay: Popular Prakashan, 1963).

Ramanujam, B.K. "The Indian Family in Transition" in *The Indian Family in the Change and Challenge of the Seventies* (I.S.I. Publications, New Delhi: Sterling Publishers (P) Ltd., 1972), pp. 22-34.

Ramu, G.N. "Researches on family in India". *Indian Journal of Social Research*, 22 (1) Ap. '81. pp. 58-75

Rao, M.S.A. "Occupational Diversification and Joint Household Organisation", *Contribution to Indian Society*, New Series, II (1968), pp. 98-111.

Rao, V.V.P and V.N. *"Marriage, the Family and Women in India"* (New Delhi; Heritage Publications, 1982)

Ross, Aileen D. "An Approach" in "Symposium on Caste and Joint Family", *Sociological Bulletin*, IV (1955), pp. 85-96.

-----. "Education and Family Change", *Sociological Bulletin*, VIII (1959), pp. 39-44.

-----. *The Hindu Family in its Urban Setting* (Indian Branch: Oxford University Press, 1961).

-----. "Changing Aspirations and Roles: Middle and Upper Class Indian Women enter the Business World" in G.R. Gupta (ed.), *Family and Social Change in Modern India* (New Delhi: Vikas Publishing House Pvt. Ltd., 1976), pp. 103-32.

Sarma, Jyotirmoyee. "Formal and Informal Relations in the Hindu Joint Household of Bengal", *Man in India*, vol. XXXI (April-June 1951), pp. 51-71.

-----. "The Nuclearization of Joint Family Households in West Bengal", *Man in India*, vol. 44 (July-September 1964), pp. 193-206.

Sen, Lalit Kumar. "Family in Four Indian Villages", *Man in India*, 45 (1965), pp. 1-16.

Sengupta, Sunil. "Family Organisation in West Bengal: Its Nature and Dynamics", *The Economic Weekly*, X (1958), pp. 384-89.

Shah, A.M. "Changes in the Indian Family", *Economic and Political Weekly*, Annual Number (January 1968), pp. 127-34.

-----. *The Household Dimension of Family in India* (New Delhi: Orient Longman, 1973).

Shah, V.P. "Mate Selection: Theories and Educated Hindu Youths' Attitude Toward Mate Selection" in Dhirendra Narain (ed.), *Explorations in the Family and Other Essays* (Bombay: Thacker & Co., Ltd., 1975), pp. 288-304.

Shahani, Savitri. "The Joint Family: A Case Study", *The Economic Weekly*, XIII (December 1961), pp. 1823-28.

Shastri, S.R. *Women in the Vedic Age* (Bombay: Bharatiya Vidya Bhavan, 1960).

Singer, Milton. "The Indian Joint Family in Modern Industry", in Milton Singer and Bernard S. Cohn (eds.), *Structure and Change in Indian Society* (New York: Wenner-Gren Foundation for Anthropological Research, 1968), pp. 423-52.

Singh, Yogendra. *Modernization of Indian Tradition* (Delhi: Thomson Press (India) Ltd., 1973).

Sinha, Durganand. "Some recent changes in the Indian family and their implication for socialisation". *Indian Journal of Social Work*, 45 (3) Oct. '84 pp. 271-86

Sinha, Raghuvir. *Social Change in Indian Society* (Bhopal: Progress Publishers, 1975).

Srinivas, M.N. *Marriage and Family im Mysore* (Bombay: New Book Co., 1942).

-----. "Foreword", *The Household Dimension of the Family in India* (New Delhi: Orient Longman, 1973).

Straus, Murray A. "Some Social Differences in Family Patterns in Bombay", in George Kurian (ed.). *Family in India - A Regional View* (The Hague: Mouton, Paris, 1974), pp. 233-48.

Suresh Kumar, P.M. "Family and Marriage Among the Keralite immigrants in Delhi". Doctoral dissertation (Jawaharlal Nehru University, New Delhi, 1981).

Sylvia, Vatuk. *Kinship and Urbanization* (London: University of California Press, 1972).

Index